A Creative Process for
Transforming Loss

GRIEF HACK

MADONNA TREADWAY

PUBLISHING

MCM Publishing
2801 B Street, Ste. 111
San Diego, CA 92102-2208
MCMPublishing.com

Book Cover and Interior Design by Monkey C Media
Content Editing by Marni Freedman
Copy Edited by Laurie Gibson
Proofreading by Adrienne Moch
Author photo by Julia Alicia Photography

First Edition
Printed in the United States of America

ISBN: 978-1-959793-01-4 (trade paperback)
ISBN: 978-1-959793-02-1 (ePub)
Library of Congress Control Number: available upon request

To Bob, Ben, Abby, and Auggie

With appreciation and gratitude for all who share stories of loss
and who embrace life with curiosity and compassion.

Contents

Content Guidance

This book explores aspects of psychology and mental health and contains depictions of loss of a loved one, job loss, identity loss, and loss and grief in general. Please read with care.

The names of individuals using the Grief-Imagic process mentioned in this book have been changed to protect their privacy and confidentiality. Any resemblance to real individuals, living or deceased, is purely coincidental.

The information provided in this book should not be used to diagnose or treat any mental health conditions. It is not a substitute for professional medical, psychological, and mental health care. If you suspect you are having a mental health problem or crisis, you should consult a mental health care doctor, provider, therapist, or counselor. You can also call or text 988 to reach the 988 Lifeline, a national network of local crisis centers that provides free and confidential emotional support to people in emotional crisis or distress, twenty-four hours a day, seven days a week.

Foreword

All of us must cope with big and small losses in life—some predictable and others shocking and unexpected. Some of us can sink into despair, and depression, or suffer debilitating anxiety due to unprocessed, suppressed grief. It can feel overwhelming sometimes. We all need a helping hand, a lifeline, a guide to help us through.

Shortly after I first met Madonna Treadway, I learned that she had lost both of her parents before the age of eight. I was struck by her warmth, kindness, and intelligence. I later learned of her decades-long journey researching unprocessed grief. She impressed me with her dedication and determination to help others suffering from painful losses.

I first had the privilege of meeting her at a program held by San Diego Writers, Ink. Madonna and I shared the same writing coach, Marni Freedman. Marni predicted that Madonna and I would become fast friends—and she was right.

As a psychotherapist, I resonated with Madonna's passion for helping people struggling with grief and loss. My first book, *Frazzlebrain: Break Free from Anxiety, Anger, and Stress Using Advanced Discoveries in Neuropsychology*, had not yet been published. Madonna too was writing her first book, *Six Healing Questions: A Gentle Path to Facing Childhood Loss of a Parent*. We encouraged each other, recognizing a shared passion for helping people manage life's toughest emotions.

Six Healing Questions provides accessible advice imbued with her warm and kind approach to grieving. It was a privilege to encourage her writing and provide an endorsement. Now I'm honored to write the foreword to *Grief Hack: A Creative Process for Transforming Loss.*

In this inviting work, Madonna shares her helpful discoveries with readers seeking ways to navigate grief's often-treacherous emotional waters. She shows you how to mobilize your imagination to help you fully understand grief. With her Grief-Imagic process, readers learn how to face their grief with warmth, compassion, and even humor. This book is helpful for both recent grief and even losses from decades past.

The author shares how to move through grief in four simple steps. In step one, she invites the reader to See It or visualize grief, to explore how it manifests in your life. Step two teaches you how to embrace grief, rather than run from it. She offers practices and insights that gently guide you through acceptance of this painful emotion.

In step three, she shows you how to integrate grief, normalizing it as a part of yourself and your history. Rather than feeling consumed or defeated by grief, Madonna shows you how to identify and incorporate it into your life in a natural way.

In the final section, she shows you how to harness grief to fuel your growth and well-being. Readers will find real-life stories and examples of how others have benefited from the use of the helpful tools in this book.

I have enjoyed employing three tools from the Grief-Imagic Toolbox: the Magic Wand, Curiosity Cap, and Flowing Pen. The Magic Wand tool is employed when you need some magic to help you go back in time, speed time up, or slow things down.

The Curiosity Cap is helpful when you feel stuck or unsure how to proceed. Like a child, you can imagine anything. The Curiosity Cap allows you to feel inspired and motivated. You can ask it questions like, "Where was I when it happened?" or "I wonder what my mom thought about that situation?" The Curiosity Cap can help you safely explore your memories and questions about your grief.

The Flowing Pen tool allows you to gain the benefits of journaling about your feelings. Madonna gently encourages creative expression and shares research about the healing effects of journaling about emotional pain, memories of loved ones, and loss.

In my work as a psychotherapist, I know firsthand how journaling helps people healthily process difficult emotions. Sometimes we need a friend, therapist, or as Madonna recommends, a Grief Hack Buddy to help us through the difficult parts. She offers helpful ways to work with your buddy, offering mutual support and effective listening strategies for a deeper connection.

Written in the voice of a warm and encouraging friend, Madonna guides the reader from initial feelings of silly awkwardness to deeper healing and connection with themselves and others. When we suppress or deny grief, it cuts us off from deeper parts of ourselves. It can even block intimacy with others.

Madonna opens the pathway to understanding one's grief with a playful, fun, creative approach. I invite you to discover your own Magic Wand, Curiosity Cap, and Flowing Pen. Muster your imagination, grab your journal, and open your mind to the dazzling magic that awaits in *Grief Hack*.

—Gina Simmons Schneider, PhD, author of *Frazzlebrain: Break Free from Anxiety, Anger, and Stress Using Advanced Discoveries in Neuropsychology*

Introduction

Dear Reader,

Loss can impact us in ways we may not fully understand. We may know that a situation or experience is hurtful, but we don't always know how to process that hurt. All too often, our culture has trained us to deny our pain, suck it up, and move on. We often try to hurry through or ignore our feelings because we associate the notion of processing pain with, well, more pain. Even if we know that the pain will resurface or show up later in our lives in an unhealthy manner, who wants to relive a painful experience when burying it seems so much easier?

This book will teach you a creative way to process your grief. This process will engage your curiosity and imagination. It can become an enlightening and sometimes playful learning experience.

Processing your grief and loss in this creative manner gives you an accessible language so that you no longer feel as if burying your pain is the easier option. Three things are going to happen. You will learn a new way to view and interact with your losses, your fear surrounding grief will shrink, and your understanding of yourself will grow.

It is worth saying that this book is for you if you have ever lost a loved one. But it is also for you if you have experienced anything like losing a job or a relationship; receiving a deeply troubling medical or psychological diagnosis; losing an identity, home, or sense of place in the world; or losing a beloved pet. In short, this book is for you if you are human.

Whatever experiences have brought you to these pages, I am delighted you are here. Just by opening the book and being willing to learn about a new approach to self-care (which I call the Grief-Imagic process), you have shown curiosity and openness. I'm excited to present to you a creative way to process these challenging transitional experiences and turn them into fuel for life.

A hack is a creative solution to a problem or limitation.

Grief Hack offers you a shortcut process that gives you a way to transform loss and grief into something helpful and self-affirming. You will enrich your life while suffering less. The Grief Hack experience can also be playful and fun, which is something we typically do not associate with loss and grief. I'm hoping this journey will change your mind and your life.

The Grief-Imagic Process: How to Walk Yourself Through Loss by Engaging Your Imagination

Grief and Loss → Engage Your Imagination → Transformation

Together we are about to travel through four steps to help you work with your grief in a uniquely creative and tangible manner. We will be activating and engaging your imagination. Most likely, you have never been asked to connect with, or view your losses, this way. The Grief-Imagic process will help you to transform your internal experience into an image you can interact with.

"An image?" you might ask.

Yes! An image.

Here's how it works. I ask the people I work with to think of their grief as an image. Then, from their imagination, an image pops out. One person I worked with saw a slippery gray snake. Another person saw their grief as a hovering black cloud. A third saw their grief as a red cartoon hammer. Other examples have included a ball of slime, a volcano, a wolf, a scary ghost, a deep well, an ogre, and a dragon.

By coming up with these images, people were able to externalize their grief and loss. Instead of grief surrounding them like a draining heaviness in their hearts, their grief was now an image—an image they would soon learn how to interact with courageously.

This book will offer you tools that will be both transformational and lasting. Even if you have never done any creative process like this before, working with your "grief image" can reduce your fear of grief, allow you to learn essential lessons from your grief, and no longer feel your grief as such a heavy burden.

Why Work with Your Imagination? What the Experts Say

Tor Wagner, director of the Cognitive and Affective Neuroscience Laboratory at CU Boulder, performed research that shows that using our imagination helps in rewiring our brain. What the researchers found is that there is a way to harness the brain's impressive power. "Your brain on imagination is a lot like reality," said *Science Daily*. The University of Colorado research reveals that our imagined experience impacts us neurologically in a positive way. The researchers had participants continuously picture phobias in a safe environment and used brain imaging to verify their findings. What they found is that picturing phobias stimulated similar brain regions as found in actual exposure. Over time, this kind of creative exposure resulted in a less fearful response. "This research confirms that imagination is a neurological reality. It can impact our brains and bodies in ways that matter for our well-being," explained Mr. Wagner.

The Four Grief-Imagic Steps

The Grief-Imagic process consists of four steps: See It, Embrace It, Integrate It, and Harness It. The "It" I'm referring to is your grief.

Here's a quick overview of the steps:

- See It → I am aware of my grief.
- Embrace It → Instead of running, I lean into my grief.
- Integrate It → I interact with my grief until it is just another part of my life.
- Harness It → My grief is now fueling my growth.

In the upcoming chapters, we will dive deeper into each step, followed by a correlating practice to help enrich your understanding.

How to Recognize if I am Grieving

"When you haven't experienced an obvious loss such as a divorce or a death, you may not even be aware that you're grieving. These losses can be secondary to a primary loss, or they can stand on their own."

—Terri Daniel, Bereavement Specialist and author

At times we get so used to carrying the weight of our daily losses that we don't recognize that we are in a greater state of grieving. It may also be difficult to recognize grief in a loved one or child. Yet, physical and emotional symptoms can indicate that a part of you is wrestling with grief. Do you feel as if you're oversleeping or can't sleep at all? Are you eating or drinking too much, working too much, or feeling like you have no energy to enjoy life? Do you feel disconnected, like you are not quite in your body, or are you experiencing a sense of being overwhelmed, like you can't handle even one more thing or you'll explode?

Take a moment to think about how grief shows up in your life or your body. Below are just a sample of physical or emotional symptoms you might be experiencing if you are in a genuine state of grief.

Physical Symptoms

- General tiredness and extreme fatigue at times
- Random aches and pains, such as headaches, neck, or back pain
- An inability to sit still, restlessness
- Shortness of breath or heart palpitations
- Loss of appetite or its opposite: excessive comfort eating
- Insomnia, fear of sleeping, or frightening dreams
- Anxiety attacks or elevated blood pressure
- Confusion or inability to concentrate
- Difficulty remembering or gaps in memory

Emotional Symptoms

- Crying often or sobbing uncontrollably
- Long-lasting irritability or losing your temper easily
- Feeling flat or often having no reaction to emotional moments
- Feeling as if you are disconnected from your body or emotions
- Racing, anxious, confused, or panicky thoughts
- Feeling a sense of hopelessness or helplessness
- Thoughts of hurting yourself
- Denying anything is wrong, despite clear evidence in your life that something is not working
- Feeling unworthy of love or any of the good that life offers
- Withdrawing from loved ones and from life itself

When to Seek Support

Seeing a medical doctor could be vital if you or someone you care about are experiencing any of the symptoms above. Especially if you are having serious thoughts about hurting yourself or others, talk with your doctor or psychiatrist to see if more therapeutic support might help or if there might be other reasons for these symptoms. You can use the Grief-Imagic process while addressing any medical concerns.

"We don't only grieve for what's missing, but also for the ways in which those losses affect our sense of self. You can experience grief over anything that feels like a loss of identity."

—George Bonanno, Psychologist and head of the Loss, Trauma, and Emotion Lab at Teachers College, Columbia University

Life's Ups and Downs—Losses Big and Small

Life provides us with lots of losses and you can address all of them using the Grief-Imagic process. While some are bigger and can be life-changing, and others may be bumps in the road, all of our losses leave an imprint on our lives. Take a moment to review the list of types of losses and how they may be taking a toll.

Types of Loss

Relationships/estrangement—when you feel a loss through a shift in the status of a friendship, romance, or family relationship.

Financial or worldly losses—when you experience a loss in your financial security. For example, losing a job or your home going into foreclosure.

Health—when you experience a lack of physical well-being such as a life-changing illness or injury, or losing a physical ability, such as no longer being able to walk or drive.

Dreams and goals—when you experience a loss that pulls you away from a desired life path/dream you had been seeking.

Secondary loss—experiences as a consequence of a primary loss. For example, due to a primary loss of losing a job you might also experience a change in status, relationships, or lifestyle.

Unacknowledged loss—this occurs when the griever is not acknowledged or when the loss itself is not recognized or when it might be veiled in shame (for example, suicide or pandemic-related grief).

"Ignoring grief is like a leak in our roof. We can take care of it now or wait as it seeps through the ceiling, gets into the walls, and warps the floors."

—Mark Liebenow, author

When most of us think about grief or grieving, most people's minds go to some notion of the grieving process that Elisabeth Kübler-Ross outlined in her book *On Death and Dying.* This grew out of her famous seminar, "On Life, Death, and Making the Transition." She theorized that there were five stages that a person facing death would travel through (though not always in the order she considered most likely). These stages are denial, anger, bargaining, depression, and acceptance. Some have mistakenly concluded that a person smoothly travels from one stage to the next, when in reality, most have a sensation of moving from one experience to another in a way that feels organic to them. For example, they may start by feeling depressed, then move to anger, then back to depression, and then stay in a period of denial for some time. Another misinterpretation is that once a person reaches the acceptance stage, they are completely done with the process and can move on. But the process of grief is more like a spiral and will continue to echo even as it lessens over time. While the sense of loss may diminish, you may still feel it. For example, I lost a beloved sibling twenty-plus years ago. When he died, I was bereft. I still miss him and occasionally feel grief over his loss, yet it is not like the initial intense pain.

What's Going on in Your Brain When You Grieve—and How the Grief-Imagic Tool Can Help

Neuroscientist and psychologist Mary Francis O'Connor has devoted decades to understanding what is occurring in our brains while we are processing grief. In her book, *The Grieving Brain: The Surprising Science on How We Learn from Love and Loss,* she discusses how our brains work as we try to come to terms with where our loved ones have gone. O'Connor explains how neural pathways work. Think of neural pathways like the grooves in the roadmaps of your brain. When our loved one was alive, for many years we traveled along these familiar pathways. For example, you hear the garage door open, and you know you are about to see your loved one. That same scenario may be repeated over and over for years. So, the groove gets deeper. And then the loss occurs. Your brain is so used to traveling down that same path, but now when you hear any sound like a garage door, it never leads to what you have come to expect, seeing your loved one. Instead, your brain is left feeling a sense of searching and yearning. This can lead to troubling feelings of pain, confusion, or overwhelm.

The way your brain was mapped out before the loss creates pain, confusion, and a sense of being overwhelmed because the old map no longer works. The amazing news is that with time and new experiences, we can rewire our brains. We can create a new map. Using your imagination and engaging the Grief-Imagic tools can help this rewiring to happen. Think of it this way. When you first lost your loved one, your brain went on a search party that never came back with any good news. There was emptiness, confusion, sadness, and pain. But we are introducing a new experience to help that search party find a new path. As you do this work, the search party heads out and finds an image it can interact with. The Grief-Imagic work is making new pathways and helping to rewire your brain.

The **SEE IT** step (I am aware of my grief) can help with confusion, acknowledging that yes, you are trying to locate something that is no longer there (at least in the physical form).

The **EMBRACE IT** step (Instead of running, I lean into my grief) can help with pain because it offers you something concrete to do. Running away never makes it go away. Walking toward it, finding meaning and understanding can, with time, help transform pain.

The **INTEGRATE IT** step (I interact with my grief until it is just another part of my life) helps ease the sense of emptiness because you are now interacting with your grief in new and creative ways. There is something to do or experience in place of that empty feeling.

The **HARNESS IT** step (My grief is now fueling my growth) helps with new feelings of joy, discovery, and hope because it works to assist the brain to rewire itself, making a new brain map—one that functions in a powerful new way.

How Different Cultures Handle Grief and What We Can Learn

In American culture, we are often taught to grieve for a brief time, suppress our deepest emotional reactions, and then seek to return to "normal" as soon as possible. Yet, if we look at cultures around the world and the way they travel through the grieving experience, it can widen our view on processing profound loss.

Each year in Mexico and throughout Central and South America, on November 1, people celebrate *Dia de los Muertos* or the Day of the Dead. *Dia de los Muertos* is considered a holiday where family and friends are encouraged to interact joyfully with their deceased loved ones. Relatives welcome back the souls of loved ones for a brief, celebratory reunion that includes parties, food, drink, and sometimes parades. The people of the community dress up in fine clothing, wear colorful skull masks, or paint their faces bright colors.

In China, many celebrate a Taoist and Buddhist tradition called the Zhongyuan Festival or The Hungry Ghost Festival. The entire seventh month of the year is called "Ghost Month." On the fifteenth night of the seventh month, it is believed that the gates of the afterlife open, and spirits are free to roam for food, entertainment, and mischief. The rituals to honor ancestors include preparing food to feed the ghosts of deceased family members, creating an altar, and burning incense. To ensure all the hungry ghosts find their way back to the underworld, fifteen days after the feast people float lanterns on water and set them outside their houses. Hungry ghosts are believed to have found their way back when the lanterns go out.

In Korea, families remember and celebrate their lost loved ones during a harvest festival called Chuseok. It's one of the most significant holidays in the country, similar to Thanksgiving, in that food is a celebratory feature and often the highlight. During Chuseok, Koreans practice Charye, which includes creating a shrine adorned with the deceased's favorite foods. On the day of Chuseok, relatives pay their respects in several ways. They wake up early and prepare a feast for their ancestors, sometimes visiting the tombs. They place a Shinwi or a memorial tablet that symbolizes the spiritual presence of their loved one. Before the feast, they bow toward the table as they offer the gifts of food to their loved ones and then proceed with their feast of traditional dishes. This yearly ritual keeps memories alive and offers a way to process ongoing relationships and emotions.

* * *

I want to reiterate that there is no one way to handle death, grief, or loss. It's helpful to learn how other cultures make the grieving experience a collective one, or create rituals to celebrate the deceased, because American culture tends to want people to process grief privately, in a finite manner, and then move on. We can learn from cultures that allow the grieving person to feel whatever they are feeling—to cry, laugh, dance, and sleep. Further, we can learn that it is possible to incorporate our lost loved one along with feelings of loss and grief into our ongoing experience of life, possibly even in a celebratory way! Established rituals can help those still alive not only to remember their lost loved ones but can also help them acknowledge and accept the natural cycle of life and death. The Grief-Imagic process might just become your go-to ritual.

What if My Loss is Recent?

If you have experienced a significant loss in the last year, you may be feeling a sense of shock, overwhelm, or exhaustion. Feeling this way is perfectly normal and understandable. Sometimes when the loss is very recent, it can be challenging to do the Grief-Imagic activities discussed in this book. You can try it, but don't be afraid to give yourself some time before diving into these creative practices. An excellent companion book is *Six Healing Questions: A Gentle Path to Facing Childhood Loss of a Parent.* In its pages, I first wrote about my growth practice around loss and grieving. I lost both of my parents before the age of eight, and while I focus on the loss of a parent at an early age, my readers have shared that the book is helpful for loss in general.

What if My Loss Happened a Long Time Ago? Am I Carrying Unresolved Grief?

If you have experienced a significant loss in your recent past, you may be able to relate these behaviors or emotional responses to your loss directly. But if you have losses older than a year and still have chronic symptoms like those mentioned above, you may be holding onto unresolved grief. Unresolved grief has to do with an earlier loss that may not have been addressed or processed. It's normal to feel overwhelmed by emotion and to decide to sidestep, swallow, or bury the feelings. Often, we assume that we are "over" earlier losses because "enough" time has passed. Yet most of us unconsciously carry around a portion of unresolved grief. It's also likely that you processed the loss to the best of your ability at that time. For example, the ability to deal with loss when you are a child is quite different from dealing with loss as an adult.

Other details that may affect how you react to grief and loss may include:

- Support available by friends, family, and coworkers
- Your physical, spiritual, and mental health at the time of loss
- Adequate or inadequate time to process your loss
- Existing cultural and social attitudes about death and grief

Maybe grief has cropped up again because another layer is ready to be processed. Perhaps grief has popped up because a current situation has triggered you. If you have had a history of loss, being around anything that reminds you of a loss is called a trigger. When triggered, you may feel like you are experiencing the original traumatic feelings again.

Unfortunately, unresolved grief can weaken your immune system and cause other health challenges that, over time, may predispose you to illness. Just because it's hard to see doesn't mean that it's gone. Before you begin, you may want to be in a safe comfortable space where you won't be disturbed in case emotions arise. The first step to removing lingering effects is to look the grief square in the face and say, "I see you."

This small but potent step can empower you and awaken something deep in your spirit. I want you to thrive because you are learning to be in charge of how you relate to your grief. One way to do this is to ask yourself the following questions.

Seven Awareness Questions:

1. Am I experiencing any physical symptoms?

    _____

    _____

2. Am I experiencing emotional symptoms? *(In other words, do I have feelings about a loss that bother or confuse me?)*

    _____

    _____

3. Do I feel a lingering sense that something is incomplete or unresolved?

    _____

    _____

4. Have I gone through a significant life change, like moving to a new job or relationship, that has stirred up an emotional response?

_____

_____

5. Do I have a secret I am afraid of or maybe feel ashamed to talk about? Is there something I am avoiding?

_____

_____

6. Do I feel blocked or stuck, as if I cannot connect to or feel my emotions?

_____

_____

7. Do I feel triggered by a recent loss that has opened old wounds?

_____

_____

If the answer is yes to any of these questions, you are one step closer to genuinely seeing your grief. It's normal to feel hesitant, shy, or awkward around your grief. Yet I am going to walk you through a process that allows you to interact with your grief in a way that will eventually feel natural and empowering.

"If we don't change, we don't grow. If we don't grow, we aren't really living."

—Gail Sheehy, author

The Tools Inside Your Grief-Imagic Toolbox: The Magic Wand, The Curiosity Cap, and The Flowing Pen

There are some fun tools I want to introduce you to that you will want to keep in your pocket while on this journey. For example, you might want a little help with a confusing image, or you may want to slow down or speed up an experience. You may want help to feel calmer or protected if you feel nervous or scared.

The excellent news is that the possibilities are endless—because you will be working with your imagination. The three tools we will work with are the Magic Wand, the Curiosity Cap, and the Flowing Pen. Let's look at each tool and discuss how you might use them. You may want to have a specific loss in mind as you discover the tools.

1. Magic Wand → Use the Magic Wand when you need a little magic intervention.

Imagine your unique Magic Wand. Imagine how it looks. Is it sparkly and full of lights, or does it look like a battle wand with a sleek leather-and-wood handle? It can look any way you want. Know that you have it with you on this imaginal expedition. The wand is there to empower you, to help you with this process. Use it in any way that feels right for you. For example, you can use it to make something appear or disappear. You can use it to speed up time. You can also use it to slow things down or freeze them. If you need a bit of magic, grab your wand.

2. Curiosity Cap → Use the Curiosity Cap when you get stuck or are unsure about how to move forward.

Your Curiosity Cap can help when you encounter obstacles in this creative process. A stopping point may be when you find your mind blank, when you can't think of anything relevant to say or write, or when you are facing a blocked memory or perhaps a time you're hesitant to revisit. Think of it as a hat that inspires your curiosity and lights up your imagination.

You can customize your Curiosity Cap. It can be wild and colorful so that you feel alive with ideas when you put it on. It can be a calming blue hat that helps you to feel more serene. It can be a child-like cap with a twirler on top; when you put it on, think of your child-like spirit of inquiry coming alive.

Once the cap is on, see if you can allow your mind to drift to any questions you may have.

Here are a few examples:

1. Where was I when that happened?

_____

_____

_____

2. What is on my mind right now?

_____

_____

_____

3. How old was I?

_____

_____

_____

4. I wonder what my mom thought about the situation.

_____

_____

_____

5. Why does this make me feel sad or angry?

_____

_____

_____

6. Does it feel safe to relive this memory?

_____

_____

_____

7. What was is it about the situation that is troublesome?

_____

_____

_____

You may be surprised at what you find when you use your Curiosity Cap. Some of your findings may be joyful, and some may be more difficult. Know that there is no hurry; you can move through your questions at a pace that's safe and comfortable for you.

3. The Flowing Pen → Use the Flowing Pen to journal when you want to think through a question, reflect on an experience, or explore an insight.

The Flowing Pen is a special pen that helps you bring forth your innermost thoughts and write them down. It will help channel your inner wisdom, emotion, and imagination. All you need is a pen, journal, blank paper, or computer. Ask yourself, *What way do I feel most comfortable writing my thoughts and feelings?*

Journaling is a very powerful and intensely personal experience. You do it just for you, and there is no way to do it wrong. You grab your journal or computer and write whatever comes to mind. Please don't censor yourself. Don't worry about grammar, punctuation, or even making any sense. This journaling time is just for you to allow what may be below the surface to be exposed to the light.

If you need help deciding what to write about, use the following prompt.

What I'm feeling right now is ...

_____

_____

_____

Once you have journaled, please take a moment to acknowledge where you are, applaud yourself for being willing to get it down on paper, and look at your state of mind without judgment. That's all—simply see it for what it is.

A few notes on using these tools:

- If you are processing several losses, use a loss that happened at least a year ago. Recent significant loss can feel very raw and emotional. It is vital to allow time and space to process your emotions and give yourself time to recover. For this practice, it is more helpful to use an older loss that is less tender.
- These tools can be the gentle beginning of your exploration. As you get more accustomed to using your imagination, let your imagination go where it takes you. You may discover unique tools to use along your journey.

The Healing Effect of Expressive Writing

Writing about emotional upheavals can improve mental health, according to James Pennebaker, a professor of psychology at the University of Texas–Austin and co-author of the book *Opening Up by Writing it Down: How Expressive Writing Improves Health and Eases Emotional Pain*. He defines expressive writing as taking time to write about a past trauma and allowing yourself to let out your deepest feelings and thoughts surrounding the trauma. Regular expressive writing, he says, "can help people sleep better, feel and think better, and have richer social lives, all of which can bolster immune function and improve health." Studies have shown that expressive writing can significantly decrease depressive symptoms (Lepore 1997) and reduce negative emotions and PTSD symptoms (Snyder et al. 2004).

On Your Own or with a Grief Hack Buddy

You can do this work on your own or with a person you trust. Some people feel more comfortable working alone. They feel freer to explore their deepest thoughts and feelings without explaining or elaborating on their musings. If this feels right to you, honor that feeling. Others feel more comfortable working with a Grief Hack Buddy, a person to travel the steps with and share any possible confusion or insights. If you decide to work with a Grief Hack Buddy, choose someone you feel safe with—someone who will allow you space to feel whatever you are feeling without judging or demeaning. You want a friend who will be open to going with you on a journey through your imagination.

Tips For Working with a Grief Hack Buddy

One person shares while the other one listens. The listener does just that, listens and witnesses without interrupting or offering suggestions. The listener is not there to solve any problem but to create a safe space for the speaker to share.

After the speaker is finished sharing, switch roles. The listener may share what they heard and ask clarifying questions. Remember that nothing needs to be solved at that moment. You do not need to fix anything. The goal is to allow yourself to express your thoughts and feelings and to be heard. If it feels right, you each can offer observations about the other's expression. Make sure you have permission to do this. Refrain from giving advice; instead, offer what you noticed. For example, I may say to my Grief Hack Buddy, "*I noticed you had a hard time talking about this,* or *you seemed wistful when you mentioned that.*" The goal is to listen, notice, and share without judgment. If you have questions, trust that they will be answered in time.

Questions That May Arise

Q: How long does it take for the process to work?

A: For some, the process is relatively short, such as a few days to a few weeks, usually when a person is able to easily conjure up and talk to their image. Answers flow naturally. Others may find some sticking points, places where they need help moving forward. Know that you don't need to push anything into place. As much as you may want them, you don't need the answers right away. Being patient and using curiosity can help move you forward gently—and you can rest assured knowing that the answers will come in time.

Q: Do I use the Grief-Imagic process just once?

A: Once you understand the process, you can use it repeatedly.

Since life is filled with change and we will continue to experience losses big and small, this is a tool you can have available and call on as you go through all the ups and downs of life.

Q: What if I'm not used to using my imagination?

A: Give it a try, even if it feels awkward at first. The truth is we imagine things all the time. We think about the future and replay the past; we daydream. We use our imaginations when thinking about what to make for dinner or when reading a book. You may not be used to using your imagination in this manner, but with some practice, it will start to feel natural, because it is.

Take a moment right now. Imagine sitting on a park bench as the most spectacular-looking purple bird flies over your head and lands next to you.

Did you see the bench? Did you see the purple bird? That was your imagination at work.

Q: What if I feel silly or weird?

A: When you experience the rewards of the process, you will get over any awkward, inhibiting emotions. Know that all your feelings are welcome as you go through this process. It's okay to laugh or cry or curse. It may also help you to engage your inner child. You can call them to come forward to play when it's time to imagine.

Q: What if the image I pick changes?

A: Since you are using your imagination, this could and does happen. Put on your Curiosity Cap and notice how it changes. *Is it bigger or smaller? Does it change color, or is it a new image?* Know that whatever shows up is there to guide you. Lean into your curiosity and let it open doors for you.

Q: What if I see more than one image?

A: As you do this imaginative work, know you are embarking on a creative journey. Like any journey, you might find yourself surprised and even delighted by the adventure. One such surprise might be that you discover more than one image for a particular loss. Or you may find a specific image for each type of loss you are experiencing. For example, when Rick began using the Grief-Imagic tool, he found that his recent job loss showed up as a slippery silver snake, while the loss of a friendship showed up as an angry buzzing bee. I asked Rick to give each one of his images a name to help him to interact more easily with them.

It's common to uncover multiple images when doing this kind of work, especially if you're addressing more than one loss.

Q: What if I begin processing deeper losses?

A: Another common experience you may have when you start working with one loss is that another more profound loss comes to revisit you. For example, Kaylee recently lost her beloved family dog, Heidi. Heidi, a lovable golden retriever, had been in her life for almost eighteen years. As Kaylee worked with the Grief-Imagic tool, the image of a deep well came to mind. The well invited her to come close and peek over the edge into the well. When she did, she found the image of an angel. The angel looked like her mother, who had passed two years earlier. Kaylee realized that she was holding both painful experiences within that well. She felt the need to sit beside the well and cry, just to let it all out. For a few months, Kaylee visited the well and began to talk to it—to ask the well how it worked. She was surprised that the well could be filled with positive memories. The angel-mother image encouraged her to pour her best memories of her mom and Heidi, her dog, into the well. Soon the well became a source of calm and loving remembrance.

Q: What if I get overwhelmed?

A: At times, working with emotions you may not have dealt with in a long time (or ever) can feel overwhelming. My advice to you is to take your time. Do your best to approach the process lightly and playfully. Remember your tools. The Magic Wand can make something disappear, shrink, or stop time. Curiosity can provide a little breather as you step back and ponder why you feel the way you are feeling. Journaling can also offer a nice respite, a time to sit and reflect. Remember that this process is your own. There is no rush, no timeline, and nothing that must happen. Whenever you feel it's too much, take a break, walk around in nature, distract yourself, or lean on your Grief Hack Buddy.

How to Use This Book

You will want to read the book in chronological order the first time you use this process. Why? Because one step builds upon another. Feel free to skip around and use any practice in any order after you have made your way through the Grief-Imagic process once.

What You Will Find in Each Chapter

Each chapter will introduce the step, provide you with some historical, cultural, or therapeutic context and provide you with three practices to help you to explore the step. Then, we'll follow three people who've gone through the Greif-Imagic process: George, Sarah, and Jan. Their stories may help you to see how others who have processed the powerful, imaginal experience that awaits you. Also, this book is filled with places for you to journal. Feel free to write all over it as you journal your thoughts, insights, questions, and discoveries.

Chapter One:
See It

See It → I am aware of my grief.

Embrace It → Instead of running, I lean into my grief.

Integrate It → I interact with my grief until it's just another part of myself.

Harness It → My grief is now fueling my growth.

"Awareness is like the sun. When it shines on things, they are transformed."

—Thích Nhất Hạnh

The first step in the Grief-Imagic process is to increase your awareness of your grief, including any feelings surrounding your loss. Your goal is to become aware of how your grief shows up in your life and acknowledge your thoughts and feelings without judging them. You'll want to do this in the same way that you might acknowledge that you are sitting on a bench, walking to work, or making dinner. You simply, consciously notice.

An example of "Seeing It" would be to recognize a behavior within yourself, like "*Oh, look at that: I never want to get out of bed anymore.*" Or, "*That's interesting; I worry that if I start crying, I might never stop."* Or, *"Huh, look at that, every time someone brings up the loss, I change the subject."*

That's all there is to it—bringing something to the surface and acknowledging its existence. This lets you shine a neutral light on a behavior, thought, or feeling and it can now be addressed.

You may find that you experience a sense of relief by allowing yourself to admit the truth of what you've been feeling but have been ignoring. We start with this step because seeing your grief and observing how it shows up can be the beginning of a beautiful transformation. "Seeing It" is vital to this process because we will lift an unexplored feeling and transform it into an image. "Seeing It" will allow you to engage with your emotions in a tangible way that you never might have before.

The step we are focusing on here involves seeing your grief as an item, a person, an animal, or an object. You may be wondering, *How does that work? How do I see my grief as an item, animal, or an object?* To start, give yourself permission to step outside your rational mind and move into a more creative, free-flowing space. You'll be prompted to close your eyes and allow your imagination to wander as you ponder the question, **What image represents my grief?**

Many people have been surprised at how quickly an image pops up in their minds. The good news is that there is no wrong way to do this. Whatever image shows up is the right one, at least for this moment. If no image shows up right away, give yourself some time or space, or simply choose one from the list below.

Possible Images List

The following are some of the images that have popped up for people doing this work. Take a look as a way to get your imagination flowing.

- A talking fire
- A soggy blanket
- A poison alligator

- Red clouds
- A rabid dog
- A pit of quicksand
- A spider
- A heavy weight
- A gnome
- An angry witch
- A running wolf
- A blanket of snow
- Smoke
- A tornado
- A vacuum cleaner
- A cartoon fox
- A volcano
- A fist
- A harsh Spotlight
- An oversized bear
- A crazy clown
- A face on a hospital
- A confused bird
- A werewolf
- An abandoned castle
- A small ship at sea
- A stomping dinosaur

Now take a moment and let your imagination run free.

PRACTICE #1:
Warming Up the Imagination

Let's continue warming up your imagination. Let's start by creating your perfect Magic Wand, a key tool in your toolbox. Remember, you can use your Magic Wand whenever you feel you need a little imaginal magical assistance—for example, if you want to make something appear or disappear. You can use it to speed up time or slow things down. Your imagination is the limit. Imagine going to your Grief-Imagic Toolbox and taking out your Magic Wand. Hold it in your hands.

What is your wand made of?

- Is it colorful?
- Does it feel light or heavy?
- Can it glow?
- Does it sparkle?
- How does it move?
- What can your Magic Wand help you with today?

_____

_____

_____

_____

_____

_____

_____

_____

PRACTICE #2:
What is Showing Up?

Let's take a moment to relax and quiet the mind. Find a comfortable spot in a quiet, safe space where you won't be disturbed for at least twenty minutes. Light a candle or turn on soft music if this appeals to you. Sit comfortably in a chair with your spine straight and your feet on the floor. Bring your journal and your Flowing Pen.

Let's begin.

Put your hand on your heart, close your eyes, and breathe in and out a few times. Then open your eyes and allow them to land on anything in the room with a soft gaze.

Next, ask yourself the question, ***What image represents my grief?***

Allow images, objects, people, items, or places to materialize. It could be a person, an animal (real or fantasy), a place, or a thing. It may take a moment for an image to come forward, or it might happen instantly. It's okay to take your time. Don't limit yourself in any way. Just sit and see what happens. Let it come to you naturally. You want to just see the image and acknowledge it.

Once you see an image, ask yourself the following questions as you observe:

- What has shown up?
- What do I see, hear, or feel?
- How would I describe the image in detail?
- What color is it?
- Does it have a particular shape?
- Is it animated or stationary?
- Is it an animal, a person, a thing, or a place?
- Does it make noise?
- What is its current setting?
- How would I describe its demeanor?

- Is it doing or saying anything?
- Is it alone?
- How do I feel about it?

_____

_____

_____

_____

_____

_____

_____

_____

_____

_____

_____

_____

_____

_____

_____

_____

_____

Once you have spent time with the image, please thank it for coming and let it fade or retreat to wherever it lives.

Practice #3:
Noticing First Interactions

You have just had your first experience with your image. Notice how you feel physically and emotionally when the image has left. Then sit with those feelings for a moment.

Use the Flowing Pen

Remember that you can use the Flowing Pen to reflect on an experience, think through a question, or explore an insight.

Take a moment to grab your journal or write in this book. Did any thoughts or feelings arise after your image has left? Do you want to see it again? Do you have any questions for your image? How did it feel to dive into your imagination this way? Can you pat yourself on the back for allowing your image to come forward? Can you feel the bravery it took to face your image in the way you did? Simply write whatever flows to you and feels essential in the moment. Write a little or as much as you want. Trust your process and go with whatever feels right to you. Remember that you can't do this exercise wrong.

_____

_____

_____

_____

_____

_____

_____

_____

"Acknowledgment of grief—well, it makes feeling the grief easier, not harder."
—Elizabeth McCracken, author

Questions That May Arise

Q: What if no image comes forward?

A: You can stop for the day, take a walk, and trust that when you are ready, an image will show itself to you. No need to feel any pressure. If you're still stuck, notice what you see on your walk. Do you see a tree that attracts you? Do you see a bird or other small animal that draws your attention? You may be able to work with one of these beings from the natural world as your image.

Q: What if an image comes forward, and I feel scared?

A: Acknowledge how you are feeling. You can also ask the image, "You are scaring me. Can you show yourself in a way that isn't too scary for me?" Also, know that you can take a break or stop anytime and return to this activity when the intense emotions have subsided. You can also work your way through this book with a Grief Hack Buddy.

Q: What if an image comes forward and says something painful?

A: Ask the image something like, "Can you be softer with me so I can be with you and learn from you in a way that's not too painful?" Allow yourself to sit with what has been said. There's no need to react or try to solve anything. You can use your journal to process any thoughts and feelings that arise.

Q: What if I don't know how to respond?

A: Throughout the book are example dialogues you can use with your image if you ever feel stuck. However, there is no pressure to respond. You are in control of this process. You can say, "I need some time to respond." Or say nothing at all. This is your process. All of this happens at your pace and at your comfort level.

Q: What if I don't feel ready to engage with my image?

A: Take a break; get into nature. Again, there's no need to rush this process. Our goal for the first step is to see and acknowledge the presence of your image—that's it.

Q: What if I feel ready to engage and want to ask some questions, and I'm trying to figure out how to start?

A: You may be ready to move to the Embrace It step. If so, see the next chapter for sample interview questions to get the dialogue started.

We're now going to follow three people who have gone through the Grief-Imagic process: George, Sarah, and Jan. The following are their experiences with the "See It" step.

George and The Fire-Breathing Dragon

George, a 41-year-old father of three, lost his favorite cousin, Dale, in a car crash two years ago. George and Dale spent a lot of time together as kids, almost growing up like brothers. They attended the same college and decided to raise their families in neighboring communities. When George went through a breakup, lost a job, or just needed to hear a friendly voice, Dale was the person he called. Dale was spontaneous and adventurous—two things George was not. Dale loved spur-of-the-moment travels, which had encouraged George to live a life filled with surprising and meaningful experiences. Without Dale, George found himself in a funk. He barely wanted to leave his house. Bereft and exhausted, George felt nearly paralyzed, unsure how to process his myriad emotions.

George sat in a quiet place in his living room and tried the Grief-Imagic practice. His grief showed up as a giant, red, fire-breathing dragon. Although he was a little scared at first, George felt the dragon's demeanor was not threatening if he kept his distance, though he noted, "It was scary and surprising. I would have thought my grief would show up as something limp and lifeless."

George noticed that he felt cautious around the dragon, yet not terrified. As he sat with it, he observed that the dragon's tail curled around the bottom of the dragon's rather large rear end in what George thought was a protective position. The way the dragon sat reminded George of his dog, Sam, who would do this when George asked him to sit.

Sarah and The Muddy Slime

Sarah had lost her mother in adolescence to cancer when she was only fifteen years old. She was raised by an aunt and in her family, going to therapy to process the loss was not encouraged. Consequently, Sarah stuffed down the grief, graduated from high school early, and went to college. Her sole focus was to lift up herself and her family economically.

She attended business school, graduated with honors, and was hired by a top company. For many years, Sarah continued to deny she was struggling with grief over the loss of her mother. If anyone asked her, she would point to all her successes. How could she be struggling if she had a position her business colleagues envied, her dream car, and had just purchased a home in a gated community?

After she broke up with her third fiancé, Sarah realized something was not quite right internally. Her previous boyfriends had told her that she was remote, cut off emotionally, hard to reach, or shut down. She had always dismissed the feedback until her last fiancé told her lovingly that he thought she had better deal with her past because he felt he could never really connect with her on an intimate level. It was then she decided to try the Grief-Imagic approach to healing.

When Sarah started the practice and considered an image that represented her grief, she said, "I don't think anything will come up. It's all sort of a blank." At first, nothing emerged. She spent a whole session where nothing came to her mind. At the second session, she noted that different images had been visiting her in her dreams. I asked her to explore and discuss any images that had shown up. She said that there was one primary image that she'd dreamed about. "It's gross," she said in a thoughtful way. "It's like an awful mess of mud-colored slime. And it's big. Really big."

I asked her if she wanted to look at or interact with it, and she shook her head "no."

"I just want it to go away, it's awful, and it smells too."

I assured her that just seeing the muddy slime was progress.

Jan and The Puzzle Pieces

Jan lost her job as a restaurant manager after a dozen years of working her way up in the corporation. She was forty-three and single. She'd started as a greeter and slowly but surely made her way into management. She enjoyed being a manager of this fun, fast-paced downtown restaurant. She truly loved the people she worked with and couldn't imagine doing anything else with her life. Then one day, the owner said he was retiring and closing the restaurant. He thanked everyone for their hard work making his restaurant dream a reality but stated he had some health issues and needed to focus on his care instead. He told the crew that a wealthy businessperson would soon be purchasing the restaurant for the property and had no interest in keeping the business going.

At first, Jan was in complete shock. She felt that the sudden closing announcement came out of nowhere. She had a little under a month to come up with another plan for her life. Initially, she felt as if it was all too much to deal with. The restaurant felt like a second home, and all the people who worked there felt like a second family. Jan could barely say goodbye to her coworkers. She handled the loss the way she dealt with most of her losses: telling herself that she didn't have the time to feel her feelings. She told herself to buck up, and that everyone in the restaurant felt terrible and if she showed them her feelings, it might impact them negatively. She thought talking about her feelings wouldn't accomplish anything.

Jan gathered the whole team together on their last day at the restaurant. While others cried, she remained stoic. While Jan understood their upset, she didn't see how crying would help. In the voice of a calm, reassuring leader, she told them that wherever she next landed as a restaurant manager, she would find a way to hire as many of them as possible. She assured the team that she would find a way to keep them together.

Over the next few months, Jan looked for a similar restaurant manager position. But nothing seemed like a fit. She'd have a job interview and either not hear back or, when she took a closer look, felt that the environment was not healthy, fun, or challenging enough for her. After six months of being unemployed, Jan was running out of money and felt desperate. A neighbor shared that the company she worked for had a position open in their Human Resources department and suggested that she apply for the job. Jan got the job. She told herself that this job would be temporary, that she would continue looking for a restaurant manager position at night during her free time. Whenever she missed her old coworkers, she'd push away the feelings and tell herself to suck it up. After all, she'd been raised by a single mother who had changed careers three times to help keep their family afloat. When her neighbor asked her if she'd mourned the loss of her old life at the restaurant, she said, "Why would I indulge myself like that? I need to look forward and keep moving."

About a year into her new job in the HR department, she noticed symptoms that concerned her. She wasn't sleeping, she was drinking several glasses of wine at night, and she often felt unmotivated to get up in the morning to go to work.

This was around the time that she and I started working together. We talked about seeing the loss of her second "home" (the restaurant and job) as just that—the loss of a second home. Though she was good at her current job and cordial with her new coworkers, it wasn't the same as the family she'd built over a decade in the restaurant's fun, fast-paced environment.

When she began doing the Grief-Imagic work, I asked her to think up an image for the grief surrounding her job loss. When we met next, she said that several images came to mind: lost puzzle pieces that had been swept under a rug and forgotten.

I asked her to sit with the puzzle pieces, to be with them, and to let them know that she saw them.

She did so and talked about imagining herself lifting up a rug and seeing the forgotten pieces under it. The pieces shimmered a bit in the light at being seen for the first time.

> *"No one ever told me that grief felt so like fear."*
> —C.S. Lewis, author of *A Grief Observed*

A Word About Fear

We all experience fear, and sometimes, that instinct may save us from harm or injury. But fear can also stop us from moving forward or processing our emotions. Notice how you tend to feel fear if you are experiencing loss or grief. Do you tense up, let your mind run away, and imagine the worst? Do you freeze? Does your mind go blank, seeming to shut down? If so, I want you to try something different. Learn about your fear. Lean into your fear. How? Notice, pay attention if this happens. Then focus on your breathing. Imagine that your fear is a child who needs comfort. Imagine that you are the adult in the room and open your arms to that frightened child. What do you say to them? How do they feel? Once you have comforted them, how do you feel?

Write about this experience in your journal.

The title of this chapter is "See It." Part of seeing your grief is being aware. Developing personal self-awareness is one way that gives us a choice about how to proceed in our lives and the world. By recognizing what's under the surface, you will be empowered going forward. Once you better understand harnessing your experience of loss and grief, you will see a pattern. Your fear and avoidance will diminish as your understanding increases. By Seeing It and becoming more aware, you will be ready for the next step, embracing it.

* * *

Congratulations for reaching the end of this chapter. Willingness to do this kind of work—looking at difficult feelings and impulses related to your grief—shows just how courageous you are. And what I'm excited to show you next is that the process of looking your grief in the face may not be as scary as you might think; instead, it can even become part of what fuels your internal growth. Ready to see how it works? Read on.

Takeaways from Chapter One

- Awareness means that, with judgment, you see how your grief is showing up in your life.

- The Grief-Imagic approach encourages you to use your imagination to see your grief as an object, a person, or an animal. Simply ask the question, *What image represents my grief?*

- Allow yourself to step outside your rational mind and move into a more creative, free-flowing space.

- Your Grief-Imagic Toolbox contains three tools:

  - Magic Wand—Use the Magic Wand when you need a little magical intervention. For example, you can use the wand to slow down and take a closer look or speed up time to envision the future.

  - Curiosity Cap—Use the Curiosity Cap when you want to enter your imagination. It helps to put it on if you get stuck or are unsure about how to move forward.

  - The Flowing Pen—Use journaling to reflect on an experience, or as you think through a question or explore an insight.

- If you feel nervous or scared, take a moment to care for yourself. Focus on your breathing, then imagine your fear as a child who needs comfort. See yourself as the caring adult and open your arms to that frightened child.

- As you move about the world while doing this imaginal work, be open to seeing your life experiences with fresh eyes. Your imagination is more active and alive and may pleasantly surprise you.

Chapter Two:
Embrace It

See It → I am aware of my grief.

Embrace It → Instead of running, I lean into my grief.

Integrate It → I interact with my grief until it's just another part of myself.

Harness It → My grief is now fueling my growth.

"Embrace your grief. For there, your soul will grow."
—Carl Jung, Swiss psychiatrist, and psychotherapist

As we have discussed, we will all experience a variety of losses over the course of our lives. There's no getting around it. Some losses will feel minor, while others may feel insurmountable. We may likely lose a job, end a friendship, grow old, or lose a loved one. Though many of us were trained to "suck it up," brush our experiences under the rug, and ignore our feelings, this step we're about to explore is going to take you in a different direction. The essence of the Embrace It step is to make space for what you're experiencing.

Embracing our grief means taking a moment to breathe while walking toward the pain. While we do this, we want to notice what we think and how we feel as we approach it.

Right about now, you might be thinking,

Ummm, why exactly should I lean into my emotional pain? Wouldn't it just be easier to ignore it and hope it goes away?

If running away and ignoring grief worked, that's the route I think most of us would take. Unfortunately, it doesn't work. When we block, disregard, ignore, or lock away our feelings about our losses, we still must face the emotions in one form or another. For example, you may deny that you feel sad, then find yourself drinking too much. Or you might ignore that you feel lonely and fall into depression or experience a long episode of apathy. Detaching from our emotions doesn't make them go away; it just transforms them into new and unique life problems.

Embracing the grief helps us to:

- Be more alive and present for the happier moments that will surely happen in time
- Connect with a rich inner life that's awaiting us
- Uncover insight or offer a perspective that can transform the way we view our lives
- Teach us how to be more compassionate and loving to ourselves

Just as we would offer compassion to a hurt child, we want to learn to love our own tender underbellies.

Why We Run

What is there about your story that you want to run from, not talk about, or bury? Is there raw emotion and possibly shame? Are you afraid of being vulnerable or exposed? I know that feeling very well. I know the feeling of not wanting to share a terrible secret because it's too painful to discuss. Too humiliating to share. Too buried to want to dig up. I lost both of my parents before I turned eight. Even at this young age, I put my head down and moved forward. I deceived myself for years telling myself I was "fine." My early loss and trauma were in the past, and I wanted them to stay in the past.

We may think that avoiding and ignoring is what's expected of us by our culture. We are trained to answer "okay" or "fine" when asked, "How are you?" Many times, after a loss, we feel far from okay. Yet, we say it to make others comfortable. It feels as if others want us to move on and get over it. Eventually, we may even start feeling like we are moving on. Sometimes we are, and sometimes we've gotten so far away from dealing with the loss and our grief that it bubbles up in other areas. Avoidance can cause emotional confusion, depression, or substance abuse. It's then that we realize that ignoring our feelings has been nothing more than a Band-aid.

I was far into adulthood before I would talk about the loss of my parents. Avoidance was how my family handled grief, and it seemed to work well for me. I took complex thoughts or emotions and stuffed them somewhere I couldn't see, thinking this was helping me move forward. In some ways, I was right. I was able to move forward. I studied hard and started a successful career. From outward appearances, it looked like I had everything. I had a good job and was upwardly mobile. Once that pattern was in place, it was hard to break out.

Yet internally, I was in a type of pain I couldn't quite identify. I was shut down emotionally but not aware of it. Relationships with my partners were unsatisfying; they felt lukewarm. I also felt that a sense of deep connection was missing. In some ways, I felt like I was living half a life.

You, too, may be experiencing some of these same struggles. As discussed in the last chapter, you may be experiencing physical or emotional symptoms that tell you something isn't right. Your first instinct may be to avoid what registers as painful and even threatening. I understand this; I've been there. However, I did break out of the avoidance loop that kept me trapped, and so can you. But I only achieved this by listening to and nurturing my curiosity.

Let's Talk About Avoidance and Curiosity

The bad news is that you (like most people) probably have a habit of avoiding what scares you. The good news is that you can change that habit. One reason to work on changing the pattern is that research has found that coping by avoidance creates anxiety and stress. It also chips away at self-confidence because it sends a message internally that you cannot manage. But by becoming curious and aware, you can act and change. Addressing the pattern may take time, so don't panic if it seems difficult at first. If you feel too overwhelmed to make this change alone, it's okay to seek out professional help, like a therapist, counselor, or coach, to assist you. Or you can do this work with a trusted friend.

This is a great time to remember one of the tools in your Grief-Imagic Toolbox: your Curiosity Cap. Remember that you can use it when you get stuck or are unsure how to move forward.

Could you put the Curiosity Cap on and explore ways you may be using avoidance to cope? Below are some questions and ideas for you to consider.

Do you have a "hidden self" you are trying to keep safe?

Have you ever felt the need to protect yourself and not share your feelings, fearing that you might be hurt or misunderstood?

_____

_____

Though it is entirely normal to feel protective of yourself and not want to appear vulnerable to the outside world, take a few moments to think of ways you may have closed yourself off in order to protect yourself. Then ask if there is one aspect of your life where you feel you can open the door to sharing who you are with the world, even to just let in a small crack of light.

_____

_____

_____

Examples of Avoidance and Why Lean In?

One tactic to avoid the upset of loss is to play it safe. You may arrange your life in such a way that you avoid further loss. For example, shying away from intimate relationships because you don't want to feel the pain of a breakup. Or you may stay in a job that doesn't challenge you because you don't want to chance moving out of your comfort zone.

If your natural inclination is to avoid and if the culture nurtures avoidance, you may wonder why I'm asking you to move in the opposite direction.

Here's why: Avoidance is only effective up to a point. Sooner or later, you will face either a situation you cannot control or a feeling that you are not living a full life. In other words, you can use avoidance for only so long. Loss is something we all experience; no one escapes it. Difficult situations or a desire to grow will come knocking on your door. You can start down a path of genuine healing by opening that door.

My experience has shown me that embracing my grief/loss is one way to show acceptance of the vulnerable parts of myself that I considered broken or damaged. Embracing this part of myself helped me address any shame I was carrying about my losses. Acknowledging my loss and grief has helped me understand that I'm not broken or damaged. Instead, I see that I'm traveling through a universal experience. Knowing this helps me feel more connected to myself and my human family.

Doing this work, leaning in, will help you to see that healing is on the horizon. I know it may not feel like it, but by acting in an unexpected way and leaning into your grief, you may experience a different and more life-affirming result.

Mark Nepo, spiritual writer, poet, philosopher, and author of eighteen books, put it this way, "Though it's understandable to be consumed with what we're going through, … When closed, we need to open. When fearful, we need to trust again. When feeling lost, we need to remember that we are in the stream of life, which is never lost."

Research on Exposure Therapy—Facing Fear and Using Imagination

There is science behind this type of work. It's what psychologists call exposure therapy.

What is Exposure Therapy?

Exposure therapy is a psychological treatment that has helped many people confront their fears. Avoiding activities, situations, people, or objects that make us fearful is normal. In the short term, we feel better, maybe even relieved. But this doesn't solve the problem, and long term, ignoring the troubling aspects of our lives can often cause the anxiety to grow. Exposure therapy helps a person gently break the pattern of avoidance.

How Does Exposure Therapy Work?

Therapists or counselors create an environment where clients feel calm, open, and safe. Next, they help the client bring what they fear into their minds to face the fear. The simple act of exposing the client to a perceived fear has been shown to reduce anxiety and decrease overall avoidance.

How is the Grief-Imagic Approach the Same or Different?

This Grief-Imagic process is similar to exposure therapy because we create a safe environment and walk you toward seeing and being with your image to reduce its negative impact on your life.

It's different from traditional exposure therapy in two ways. One, you can do the Grief-Imagic method on your own: just you, your imagination, and a journal. Exposure therapy is usually done with the guidance of a professional therapist. Two, by using the imagination as our primary creative power we will move beyond exposure and into transformation. (You will see this more in chapter four.) The Grief-Imagic process opens the door to exploring how your grief may be a transformative force in your life.

"The act of experiencing something new—or even doing something typical for you, but in a different way—can all generate these new brain cells…. We want to constantly be using new paths and trails and roads within our brain."

—Sanjay Gupta, chief medical correspondent, practicing neurosurgeon, and associate professor of medicine at Emory University School of Medicine

Let's walk through the process and use some of our tools that can help you along your journey.

The Magic Wand

One way to use your Magic Wand is if you feel nervous or scared in the presence of your grief image. Instead of following an impulse to flee and run from it, imagine gently moving toward your image with your Magic Wand. Imagine that your Magic Wand has the power make your image less scary. It has the power to make your image smaller, change its color or shape. The Magic Wand has the power to put your image in a container and seal it if you wish.

Here's how Jessica used her Magic Wand. Jessica was grieving the loss an internship she had applied for. She imagined her grief as a giant spotlight that chased her, exposed her, and made her feel naked. By working with her Magic Wand, she transformed the spotlight into a ray of warm sunlight. The sunlight was inviting and healing, like a warm hug. Jessica imagined walking into that light while feeling friendly, peaceful energy surrounding her. Whereas at first she'd found herself wanting to run and flee in panic, in time she found herself wanting to stay and be warmed by the light.

Having the Perspective of Time

You may be thinking that it's easy to say that perspective will come in time—but harder to trust and allow it to happen. Your concern is valid. It can feel awful when you're wading through a new loss or disappointment. It may seem like you will feel this way forever. Know that it will pass. The key ingredient is time. As time passes and you work through your feelings, you will gain perspective and have a clearer vision. Patience is hard but the security of knowing that you have a technique to help move through the process will help ease your mind.

PRACTICE #1:
Where Does the Loss Sit in My Body?

First, let's take a moment to relax and quiet the mind. Find a comfortable spot in a safe space where you won't be disturbed for at least twenty minutes. Light a candle or turn on soft music if this appeals to you. Sit comfortably in a chair with your spine straight and your feet on the floor. Bring your journal, a pen, and your imagination.

Then ask yourself, *Where do I feel the grief in my body?*

You might get a sensation that the grief is sitting in the middle of your chest, on your heart, or your shoulders. If you don't know, ask yourself, *Where do I notice the sensation when I imagine the loss I'm experiencing now?*

As you locate the sensation, pay attention to what body part feels heavy, tight, dense, or constricted. It may be that a part of your body or a place in your body feels uneasy or uncomfortable.

Ask, *Am I experiencing this sensation in my chest, throat, or shoulders?* Is it a powerful or a subtle sensation? Does it have a shape or color? Now take a mindful breath in and out.

Envision that feeling in your body softening as you continue to breathe. Take a moment to gently explore that feeling before moving on. Then imagine how it would feel if the sensation was released. For example, if you feel a sense of heaviness on your chest, imagine someone lifting that weight off your chest.

Or if you feel a sensation of tightness in your throat, again take a moment to gently explore that feeling. Whatever you are feeling, remember not to judge, just notice. Then imagine taking a breath that clears out the tightness so that you can now breathe easily.

Do you notice any changes in your body?

Does your chest feel lighter? Does your throat feel more open? Is there any other sensation that gets your attention?

As we end our meditation, express gratitude to your body and any feelings you have. Afterward, come back to the room and when you are ready open your eyes.

How do you feel? Does your body feel lighter, more relaxed, or changed in any way? Pay attention to any emotions that surface. Make a few notes either here or in your journal about your experience.

_____

_____

_____

_____

_____

_____

_____

_____

_____

_____

_____

_____

_____

_____

_____

_____

_____

Example of Practice #1: Kara's Story

Kara had to rehome her beloved dog, Mr. Bones, after fourteen years of being best friends. Her landlord decided to enforce a no-pet policy. It broke her heart because Mr. Bones was a best friend. He loved to run, so she found a home for him at a ranch where they would take good care of him. Kara missed Mr. Bones, and it seemed like she would never get over the sad feeling she carried with her. She wrote the following in her journal:

Kara's first journal entry:

I feel the grief right in the middle of my chest and in my solar plexus. I am trying to let the pain go, but it just sits there. My muscles feel very tense, especially in my neck and shoulders. I am going to take a minute to imagine the feeling leaving my neck and shoulders.

Kara's second journal entry:

Wow, that was kind of interesting and unexpected. When I imagined the feeling leaving me, I felt as if bricks were being taken off my chest, one by one. Then I felt lighter. My neck and shoulders still feel tense, but that heaviness in my chest has diminished, and I can breathe easier.

PRACTICE #2:
Make it Real (Bring it into Actual Physical Form)

For this practice, you'll want to take your image, which up until this point has only existed in your imagination, and make it a physical, tangible item you can hold. For example, Dan's image was a big red dog. He went to the craft store and bought a ceramic dog that he could paint. He painted it red, then placed it on his kitchen table. Alana's image was a volcano. Walking on the beach, she found a rock that looked mountainous and volcanic. She decided that this rock would represent her image. She took it home and placed it on her desk.

Elise was working with an image of a snake and made one out of clay. Tom's image was of a black panther, and he found a black rock symbolizing the panther. He kept the rock by his bedside so he could see it daily and he would sometimes talk to it, asking questions.

There is no wrong way to do this practice. You can select or create anything you want as a physical representation of your image. Other examples are a pill bottle, a mug, a figurine, a framed picture, a plaque, a book, something made of clay, a watch, something from nature, or a small found object. You could take a walk in nature as you think about your image and look for something in your surroundings—a feather, a rock, a branch, or whatever you may find.

Once you have the physical manifestation of your image, place it somewhere you'll see it on a regular basis, like a bedside table or a shelf in your living room. You may likely find that once it is in physical form, your image becomes less scary, and you can commune with it—or even incorporate it into your daily life. Feel free to interact with it or ignore it. If you feel drawn to interact, you can talk to it, ask it questions, or just sit quietly with it. You can use your journal to jot down any ideas or revelations. You get to decide how much interaction you want to have with the physical object and how long you want to spend with it. These tactile objects can often become a comfort and shortcut to tap into your inner life. I have some that have been with me for years and feel like companions as I move through life.

PRACTICE #3:
Be With It

You can do this practice using your imagination or with your physical representation of the image. Having your physical representation is handy because it can call upon your senses in its own way.

Place your feet on the floor and feel grounded. Take three calming breaths. Inhale to the count of four.

One—two—three—four.

Then exhale to the count of four.

One—two—three—four.

When you're ready, pretend you are watching a movie of your image, and you are sitting side by side in a neutral space like a park or your living room. If you have a physical representation of your image, have it with you while you do this practice.

Picture the two of you just sitting peacefully, with no harm coming to you.

Stay in that safe, peaceful place for two minutes or longer.

When you are ready, open your eyes and check in with yourself.

How are you feeling?

Did you notice if anything changed? Did you get closer to the image, or did the image get closer to you? Did the image talk to you? Did you respond? What impulse did you have toward the image as you sat together? Did you notice the image moving or changing in any way?

Now notice the image in detail. Where is it? What color is it? Is it familiar? Have you seen this image before? What is it doing? Does it acknowledge your presence?

Does it have anything it wants to tell you or show you?

Do you feel that the image needs to be contained?

Do you want to talk with the image or be quiet with it?

When you feel done, return your attention to the room, open your eyes, and wiggle your toes.

Record what happened in your journal or on the lines below.

Read your journal entry the following day. As you read, notice how your body feels. Does your body feel any different? If so, describe the difference.

_____

_____

_____

_____

_____

_____

_____

_____

_____

_____

_____

_____

_____

_____

_____

_____

Questions That May Arise

Q: What if my image feels overpowering?

A: If you feel overwhelmed or overpowered by the presence of your image, don't panic. It's a normal reaction and can be handled. You can stop and go to a trusted friend or mentor to seek advice or help. You can also use your Magic Wand to help calm the situation. For example, Jenny's image was a toxic gas. Sometimes she would see it float around her in a threatening way, which she found very scary. When I asked her who might be able to help contain the gas, her father came to mind. She envisioned him using a vacuum cleaner to suck away the gas and keeping it in the vacuum bag. If the gas ever threatened to leak out, her father would tap on the vacuum cleaner, and it would remain safely contained.

Q: What if I start feeling a flood of traumatic memories?

A: If you are experiencing your image and suddenly feel flooded with memories, take a breath, and take a step back. Ask yourself if you feel safe enough to allow your feelings without being overwhelmed by anxiety or fear. If you are alone and feel safe, go ahead and let the feelings come a little at a time. One idea is to imagine these memories in an eye dropper. You can release them one drop at time to slow things down. Then record the experience in your journal. If you are concerned but don't think you can stop the flood of emotions, stop and reach out for help from your Grief Hack Buddy, a therapist, or a trusted friend before you proceed. You can also check in on grief-support groups online. Know that you can always lovingly stop the process and distract yourself by simply going outside in nature or perhaps watching a funny video. You can revisit these memories later with a Grief Hack Buddy or a mentor: an actual person, a fantasy, or a mythical one.

A Quick Assessment, 1 to 10

When you feel yourself getting a little emotional or overwhelmed, take a breath and rate how you feel on a scale of 1–10. One is feeling very safe and not overwhelmed at all, and ten is very scared or totally overwhelmed. A general rule is that a rating of number five tends to feel manageable, but you may want to stop working with your image at that point and remember to take a healthy break anytime you exceed the number five.

Q: What if my image seems out of control?

A: Remember that you have control and can find a way to contain your image. When using your imagination, your options will be endless. For example, Jake lost the use of his right leg while serving in the military in Afghanistan. The image he came up with for his grief was a wolverine on the prowl. Sometimes he felt that wolverine might run out and cause chaos. By using his imagination and asking for the help of a mentor, Jake brought in his mother, who showed him how to pick up the wolverine and place him on an isolated island. This way, the wolverine could run free and wild but could not hurt anyone.

The Flowing Pen: Reflecting

Find a comfortable spot in a quiet, safe space where you won't be disturbed. Sit comfortably in a chair with your spine straight and your feet on the floor.

Once you are comfortable, invite your image by name (if it has one). Do you still see the same image? Do you notice any changes? Take some time to be with your image. How do you feel? Do you have anything you want to express? If you speak to the image, does it respond in any way?

_____

_____

_____

Is the image doing anything? Notice details. Where is it? Is it in your environment, a forest, by the water? In your mind's eye, get a little closer to your image. How does it react? Do you notice any changes? Does your image have anything to say to you or to show you?

Open your eyes and wiggle your toes when you feel complete. Allow a few minutes to reflect, and then record what happened in your journal with as many descriptive details as possible. Be sure to write about how it felt to be closer to your image.

_____

_____

_____

_____

_____

_____

_____

_____

_____

_____

It's helpful if you do this practice at least three times in the next week. By doing this you keep your image and your grief alive in your imagination as you lean in and embrace them. When you record in your journal, pay attention to the changes, if any, in your image and the changes in the way you feel about your grief.

Another plan is to do this three times a week for three weeks if you want to incorporate this as an ongoing practice.

If at any time you feel overwhelmed, reach out to a mental health professional.

What You May Find Along the Way

Imagination is boundless, so you may want to be prepared
for anything to happen. For example, you may find the
following about your grief image:

- The images live in another dimension.
- You can't always tell the image what to do.
- It's common to think that the image has more power
  than you think it has.
- Some images feel familiar.
- Some images may relate to your dreams.
- The image may have something to tell you or to show you.
- You may be fascinated and attracted to your image.
- Scary or unusual images that get your attention may
  want to feel heard or seen.
- Some images may be surprisingly obedient and cooperative,
  and even funny.

George and The Fire-Breathing Dragon

George, the 41-year-old father of three who lost his cousin Dale in a car crash, felt profoundly saddened and was unsure about how to process the many painful emotions he was experiencing. As a refresher, George's grief showed up as a giant, red, fire-breathing dragon named Red. George didn't particularly like the dragon, yet he felt like it might not hurt him if he kept it at a safe distance. During his first connection with Red, George observed how Red sat with his tailed curled around him. He also noticed that sometimes a tiny flame would come out of his mouth, but the flame didn't reach him.

I asked George to imagine sitting by Red again during the second practice. George said he was having a hard time picturing that and thought he would try the "make it real" practice. On the way home that night he went to a gift shop and found a small glass dragon that resembled Red. He purchased it and then carried the glass dragon in his pocket. In the morning he placed Red by the coffee maker.

At our next meeting, he brought in the glass dragon. Red was a figurine about two inches from head to tail and about the same height and felt smooth to touch. I asked him if he thought it might be easier to imagine sitting beside Red now. George took a moment and settled in. He said he could see Red and Red was standing, but not in a menacing way. George decided to sit for a while until he noticed that the dragon sat down.

I asked George if there was anything about the dragon that could be helpful to him. He thought for a long moment, then responded, "I know it sounds weird, but I'm starting to feel like I know him, and he might know me. He feels familiar."

I asked if there was anything else he was picking up. George continued, "Well, this is even more strange—I'm getting the feeling that he may like me."

George sat with the dragon alongside of him and allowed the more pleasant feelings to increase, then he spoke. "Red wanted me to know that dragons symbolize strength and are associated with magic. I told Red I could use some magic right now."

George's face relaxed, and I could tell he had made real progress regarding Red. When he spoke his name, he seemed more intrigued rather than nervous.

I asked him if he felt comfortable meeting with Red every day at the same time for a week. George agreed to do that and to report back on his progress.

Sarah and The Muddy Slime

Sarah, thirty-seven, who had lost her mother to cancer as a teenager, had been practicing the Grief-Imagic approach for about three weeks. At her next session, she told me that she still didn't understand the purpose of the exercise and that she felt like the big ball of gross-smelling brown slime was potentially dangerous for her. I asked her to describe it.

"It's like a blob—like in that old movie, *The Blob*, only it's much, much bigger. It's almost as tall as a building and just as wide."

She also shared that she didn't like thinking about it. She said that sometimes when she looked right at it, she felt upset, maybe even a little claustrophobic. She had the urge to run away fast.

I asked her where she felt grief in her body. She responded that she didn't feel much of anything.

I asked her if she might be open to sitting down next to the slime. If instead of running, she might be willing to be next to it for a moment, like a detective, and figure it out a bit more.

She shook her head "no." Sarah said she just wanted it to disappear into oblivion. I asked if she thought it might disappear. She shook her head "no" again.

Seeing her discomfort, I asked her if there might be a way to contain the slime.

"Like what? Like putting it in chains, maybe? No, it would slip through. And if I put it in a place like a prison, I'm afraid it might leak through the cracks in the walls and the doors. It's unstoppable."

I asked her to stay with it for a moment longer to see if there was anything in the whole world that could contain it.

"Wait, I think so. What about an impenetrable acrylic box? What if we put the blob in the box and secured it with an extra lock?"

That sounded like a good solution. As we talked more about this, Sarah said the slime was no longer the size of a building, it was shrinking.

Sarah imagined the slime in a big acrylic box for the next few days. She imagined the blob as being securely tucked away, unable to get to her. When she was ready, I asked her if she thought she could sit next to the acrylic box. Though a little nervous, she practiced being with the blob by simply sitting next to the box. She expressed feeling brave. At the end of that session, I asked her where she felt her grief in her body? She said she felt it right in the middle of her chest, like a weight pressing on her.

Jan and The Puzzle Pieces

By our third session, Jan was still having trouble sleeping. She reported that she sometimes felt confused and lost while driving to work. Jan said that sometimes, it felt like she was going the wrong way on the freeway. She still wanted to drive downtown, to her old restaurant. I asked her if she had seen the puzzle pieces lately. She said they came and went but wasn't sure what they were about. She said she mostly did not want to think about it or about that time in her life and was afraid she would get too sad. At this point, we began to work with step two—Embrace It. I asked her what it would be like if she leaned into the memories instead of running from them. At first, this thought troubled her, but she agreed to think about it.

The following week Jan decided that when she was experiencing a troubling emotion or memory, she would do her best to stay with it and not ignore it. That night, the puzzle pieces did appear before her as she was going to sleep, but she noted that they were "somehow really far away and hard to see." She woke up in the middle of the night, feeling compelled to do the "make it real" practice. She went to her closet and pulled out an old jigsaw puzzle. Jan took her time, fitting and then gluing ten puzzle pieces together. She let it dry overnight and then put it on a ceramic plate from the restaurant. She kept the plate by her bedside. Since the puzzle pieces first appeared, Jan had mixed feelings about them. Yet, when she woke up and used the "make it real" practice she began to feel a shift. She felt the puzzle pieces on the plate easier to relate to and she liked holding the plate.

The next time we spoke, I asked her to work with the Curiosity Cap and the Flowing Pen the next time the puzzle pieces showed up, to see if she could move closer to the puzzle pieces and hear what they might have to say. The next time they appeared, she held the puzzle pieces glued to the plate and asked them questions. She said she felt a little funny at first but then it didn't seem silly at all. She described her experience like this:

> "The puzzle pieces showed up when I was making dinner. So, I turned off the stove for a minute, grabbed the plate and my journal, and decided to get curious about my image. I asked the puzzle pieces, 'Hey, where are you?'

I heard them say that they had been scattered underneath a rug. At first, I wanted to stop and not continue the conversation, but I felt a gentle nudge to lift the rug. As I lifted it, I found it to be moldy and dusty. The pieces seemed tattered, and it may sound weird but some of them were crying. I didn't know what to do next. Then I remembered what you said about asking questions when I felt stuck, so I asked them why they were so upset. One piece said that the pieces were all my restaurant friends and coworkers. Another piece said that I'd been lying to myself. The restaurant family was not just my second family—it was my most important family. At that moment, I realized I was terribly lonely. The truth was that I was not in touch with my mom, dad, or older sister, I wasn't married and didn't have kids, so when I came home at night, I was returning to an empty house. Also, my relationship with my current group of coworkers was just not the same as my old bond with my restaurant family. I realized that I didn't enjoy their company that much and felt they didn't have the best sense of humor. I often found myself turning down their invitations for lunch or drinks. Truth be told, I found them a bit stiff and unsociable.

"I grabbed my journal and began to write about loneliness. I allowed myself to cry. I had been avoiding that cry for a year. Even though I felt sad, it also felt good to feel the sadness. I had been experiencing this daily but didn't want to admit it.

"It suddenly seemed so clear that I wasn't trying to connect with anyone at my new job. In the back of my mind, I kept thinking I would return to the restaurant, and magically, my old life would all be restored. Like, all the puzzle pieces would magically put themselves back together."

* * *

At this point, you have met, leaned into, and maybe even embraced your grief. I know it is an ongoing process. Yet, you have challenged yourself. You're on your way to decreasing the power of uncomfortable feelings and your impulse to avoid them. Your heart has opened to possibility. You are blooming despite the difficulty. You are using your grief to enrich your life. I wish I could wrap my arms around you and celebrate with you.

Takeaways from Chapter Two

- We tend to run from our grief; I ask you to walk toward it.
- Walking toward your grief means acceptance. It means you no longer feel like a victim and are willing to adapt.
- Avoidance is common. Our culture tends to nurture avoidance behavior. Most Americans have a habit of avoiding what scares us. The good news is that we can change those habits.
- Leaning in or walking toward your grief will bring insight, growth, and surprising revelations.
- Be gentle and compassionate as you allow yourself to express anything that comes to mind.
- Be willing to ask for help.
- Remember your Magic Wand. It can help you stop and take a closer look at your grief without fear. Freeze the image and examine it more closely. You may discover new insights or experience different sensations. Remember to breathe as it will help you stay centered and calm.
- Time helps. As time passes and you work through your feelings, you will gain perspective and have a clearer vision.
- If you get scared or your image seems out of control, imagine what or who would calm the image. Then include those helper(s) in your interactions.
- Leaning into your grief helps you become aware of your courageous self. It will become easier the more you do it.

Chapter Three:
Integrate It

See It → I am aware of my grief.

Embrace It → Instead of running, I lean into my grief.

Integrate It → I interact with my grief until it's just another part of myself.

Harness It → My grief is now fueling my growth.

In the previous step, Embracing It, we took time to sit with the grief, acknowledge it for what it is, and even lean into it a bit. We tried not to block any feelings and instead allowed ourselves to feel what we felt at any moment. We did this to connect with our rich inner lives, accept ourselves and our myriad of emotional states, and uncover insight or offer a perspective that could transform how we viewed our lives.

The next step in the process is to integrate your loss. What this means is that you will interact with your grief until you feel like it is just another part of you. The process is empowering because you can move from where the pain feels throbbing and active—like a fresh cut, to where it feels softer and more manageable—like a cut that has had time to heal. It's still there, but it doesn't hold the same power over you that it might have at one time.

Integrating your loss may be a new kind of experience for you, one that may feel messy or hard to measure at first. Stick with it. I have noticed that even though healing is happening, it may be hard to see or feel at first. Moving through this step can be very intuitive. Follow your gut. If you need to slow down, slow down. If you need extra support, it's an excellent time to reach out. You will know the integration process is working because you will start to feel better. You may feel lighter, less troubled, or less triggered. You may also feel more open to new feelings and experiences. When the loss is integrated, it no longer holds the same hefty charge. In other words, it doesn't feel as painful as it once did. You can see it within yourself and know it's there, but it doesn't stop you from living your life. It's just another aspect of yourself. It's like another tile in the mosaic of you.

Reasons to Integrate Your Loss

- Developing a radar to assess any gain from a loss will allow you to acknowledge your growth.
- Increased awareness of your strengths and emotional makeup can boost your sense of self.
- Gaining a feeling of personal responsibility and losing a feeling of victimhood can help you feel empowered.
- Remembering and celebrating your lost loved ones without apprehension may decrease pain and increase joy.
- Reducing your anxiety in the face of difficult situations may help you feel more confident and self-assured.
- Integrating your loss may allow you to be a role model for others who wish to keep memories of their loved one alive.

What Integration Looks Like in Everyday Life

Unconsciously or consciously, we often gravitate toward the work of integration. It may look like writing about a loved one or a loss, teaching a child an old family recipe, creating an altar to celebrate a loved one's life, taking a trip to a departed loved one's favorite place, naming a child after a lost loved one, or painting, drawing, or making a creative tribute based on the loss. In this chapter we are focusing on the work of integration by using an image while allowing yourself to be open to myriad ways that integration may naturally occur in your life.

Kay's Story of Integration

Kay lost her father, Manuel, about eight years earlier. She and her husband, Al, have a teenage daughter named Sonya. One night the three of them were talking about Grandpa Manuel. They were missing how the whole family, including their loud and boisterous Uncle Jorge, used to gather for Grandpa Manuel's big meals. They all wondered why it had been so long since they had connected as a family. They talked about how they missed a dish that Grandpa used to make using cactus, or *nopales*, as the main ingredient.

Inspired by this realization, Kay felt compelled to buy a cactus to put on her patio. She placed the cactus in a beautiful pot and set it next to the table where she would often drink her morning coffee. She loved sitting next to the cactus, sipping her coffee, and looking out over the canyon.

One morning, Sonya joined Kay on the patio and said, "Mom, why don't we make a few of the *nopales* recipes—do you think you can remember them?" They called family and friends for the next few weeks and pieced together their favorite recipe, an exotic Ensalada de Nopales. On a Sunday night, the three took turns chopping, frying, and mixing until they brought the dish to life. They shared it while sitting on the outdoor deck, next to their cactus plant, while telling stories about Grandpa Manuel.

At the end of the meal, Sonya stated, "Mom, Dad, I think I want to make a family recipe cookbook with all the cactus recipes. Tomorrow I will call

Uncle Jorge. Then maybe we can have everyone over for a big feast." After her daughter walked away, Kay smiled to herself, feeling her father's spirit very much alive in their home.

What's Going on in Our Brains During New Experiences

While we used to believe that the brain was a fixed organ with brain cells that died off, we now know about neuroplasticity, or the brain's ability to restructure itself. When you are in the process of learning to do something new, the neurons in your brain are forming new connections. This process of learning something new means you are rewiring your brain.

Mary Francis O'Connor encourages people to open their lives to new experiences and to come up with new horizons. She states that "by giving people the support and encouragement, sometimes even permission to engage in new behaviors, their brain does learn that life is full of many possibilities."

Further, recent studies show that new experiences can stimulate a rush of dopamine. Our pleasure centers are triggered with fresh input and new ways of experiencing the world. So, the research is clear: new experiences help to rewire your brain—and make you feel good in the process.

A More Tangible Way to Think About It: Composting

I'm guessing you are familiar with composting. By taking table scraps or food waste and providing the right environment, it decomposes, and then you have useful fertilizer. It has changed form slightly and now has a valuable purpose. If you consider that your grief may be able to transform similarly, you may approach it with a different view.

Your grief and disappointment—just like table scraps—require certain conditions and time to change into something you value. Time is part of the process, and intent is another. If you understand this, you will not feel as distraught and confused while processing your grief. Instead, you may be more open to the transformational process that is occurring within you.

A Word on Being Intuitive During This Step

You may rely on your intuition regularly, or this might be one of the first times you're working to grow a stronger connection to your intuition. Wherever you are currently regarding intuition, you can use the following steps to help you connect to and enhance your intuitive process.

1. Take a moment to quiet your mind.
2. Name the feeling that is coming up for you.
3. Allow yourself to feel that feeling.
4. Ask for directions. For example, you may wonder if you should slow down or lean into a slightly upsetting feeling. As you ask the question, pay attention to what comes up for you. You will often get an initial hit or a gut feeling without having to think too much. Try following that feeling.
5. Praise yourself for following your intuitive feeling, knowing you can trust yourself as your highest guide.

Nayeli's Story

Nayeli worked with high-risk teens as a counselor at a drug and alcohol treatment center. She had planned to stay at the job for about a year and then move on to specialize in clinical testing for schools.

When her company lost funding, she was laid off. She found the loss devastating. She loved her work, loved working with the kids, and felt passionate about making a difference. Yet the loss was real; the position no longer existed. She took some time to mourn the missing part of her life. She talked to friends and loved ones about her fondest memories of the job. She thought about all her clients and how much she would miss seeing them regularly. She thought about a challenging client, Denise, who had made significant changes during their time together.

Following her intuition or a sense of a calling from within, Nayeli thought about what she really loved about the job. She realized that it wasn't just this particular job that she missed; it was specifically working with at-risk youth.

She no longer felt like she wanted to specialize in clinical testing. On a hunch, she began to explore master's degree programs that specialized in working with and serving at-risk youth.

As she moved on in her career, the memories of that first special counseling center, Denise, and all her first clients, were with her, integrated into her life forever.

Check-In Questions to Track Your Progress

One way to track your progress during the integration process is to do a quick check-in before and after the practices. During this check-in, assess how your image is currently impacting you. See if your image feels like a positive force in your life, a neutral force in your life, or a warning sign. This assessment will help you to understand your current relationship with your image and the grief behind it.

After the practice, you can do the same check-in. Answering these quick questions can help you understand how the integration process is materializing in your life. You may notice that doing the practices will slowly move the needle away from feeling as if your image is an opposing force and more toward feeling that it is a neutral or positive force in your life. If you feel that you are experiencing a warning sign, this is a great moment to pay special attention. Fears may come to the surface and likely, you will unearth some insights about your grief.

Before doing the Integrate It practices, take a moment to answer the following questions.

Is the image a positive force in my life?

_____

_____

_____

Is the image a neutral force in my life?

_____

_____

_____

Is the image acting as a warning sign in my life?

_____

_____

_____

There are no wrong answers, and you do not need to think deeply here. We are looking for your initial gut check to see if your relationship to your image feels positive, neutral, or like you are experiencing a warning sign. It's also okay if you don't know how you feel about the image at this moment. Be patient with yourself as you take these essential steps to integrate your loss.

Practice #1:
Invite Your Image to Interact with You

In the last chapter we worked to make your image physical and to just sit and be with your image. Now we are going to take the next step and invite the image to connect with you, to become a part of your life. This practice contains three parts: centering, sending out the invitation, and practice sitting in non-judgment.

Centering: Before we send out this invitation, let's first work on centering your body so you will feel a sense of inner balance while doing this exercise.

Have you ever noticed how your body reacts when you try to avoid something? You may tense up, feel a pit of anxiety churning in your stomach, or get a headache.

Take a quick moment to try something right now. Stand up and imagine that there is something before you that you do not want to approach. Notice what happens in your body. Do you want to lean back, push, or pull away? Consider how this movement may put your body out of balance.

Now re-center yourself and think about something you are drawn to, and that you want to approach. Do you notice how your body is standing in a position of strength? This is because you are in balance, with your ribs over your pelvis, and have freedom of movement. Taking a few moments to center yourself can help you to feel grounded. Remember to do this in a safe place where you won't be distracted.

Sending the Invitation: Imagine sending an email or a written note to your image, inviting your image to come forward to connect with you. The note might simply say, "I would like to connect with you, would you be open to that?" Or it might say, "I'm nervous but I think I want us to talk, can you come meet me?" Think of what feels natural to you. You can express fear, hesitancy, reluctance, or openness.

If your image is reluctant, there is no rush. You can put aside the work and try again later. In my experience, if you are persistent, the image eventually agrees to connect.

Mark's Invitation.

Mark, a twenty-four-year-old graphic artist, lost his ability to use his right hand after a car accident. His image was a spinning tornado, and he was incredibly reluctant to invite it to come closer. Here is what he wrote to his image. (Note that even though he was unsure about the experience, he kept the door open.)

> "Dear Spinning Tornado, you suck. I'm really mad at you because I feel like you are keeping me off balance, in a whirlwind of angry emotions. I don't really want to be around you, like at all. But I also feel like I'm really tired of dealing with you the way you are and I'm wondering if we can talk to see if you can simmer down a little, maybe be less aggravating in my life. I will try to be mellow when we meet, open to what you have to say. Will you come talk to me?"

Practice Sitting in Non-Judgment: Imagine yourself walking toward the image. Feel grounded to the earth, safe and protected as you get closer. Now, just as you did in the last chapter, I want you to try sitting with your image and try accepting it for what it is. Imagine that you are experiencing no judgment and feel no need to run away. You are happy to be with the image while experiencing a peaceful co-existence.

It may help to think of a moment when you have co-existed with a pet or a friend. You may not have been interacting at the time, but just sitting together calmly and peacefully, aware of the other's presence and feeling neutral about it. Try to do that with the image—neutral, calm co-existence.

Grab your Flowing Pen and take a moment to reflect on how it felt to extend the invitation and to practice being with your image in a non-judgmental way.

_____

_____

_____

_____

Practice #2
Interview Your Image

Once you feel more comfortable being with your image, it's time to take the next step in the Grief-Imagic process. First pay attention to how you feel. It's okay to feel a wide variety of emotions; fear, curiosity, anger, frustration, hopefulness—or you may be surprised and feel a measure of compassion. You may also find yourself feeling a bit stuck. Remind yourself that you are in no hurry and that everything you need to know will reveal itself in time.

* * *

Place your feet on the floor and feel grounded. Take three calming breaths. Inhale one—two—three—four. Then exhale to the same count.

When you are ready, pretend you and your image are sitting side by side in a neutral space like a park or living room. If you have a physical representation of your image, you may want to have it with you while you do this practice.

Picture the two of you sitting peacefully, with no harm coming to you.

Stay in that safe, peaceful place for two minutes.

When it feels right to begin a dialogue with your image, here are some sample questions to start the conversation. The goal is to continue to engage your curiosity and allow yourself to express whatever wants to be expressed.

- What do you want?
- Why are you here?
- Where do you live?
- How do you feel?
- Do you need anything?
- Did the image respond?

If so, take a moment to write down what you heard.

Olivia's Interview with Her Image (Dialogue #1)

Olivia had lost her sister to breast cancer the previous year. Olivia's image was of a black hole that she feared might swallow her up. She imagined the black hole was sitting next to her in a tranquil green park. Here is how her interaction went with the black hole:

Olivia: Hello, Black Hole.

Black Hole: Hello.

Olivia: So, I'm curious why you are here. What is it that you want?

Black Hole: I'm here to scare you. Is there anything scarier than a black hole?

Olivia: I don't think so. I don't even want to look at you too closely. Why do you want to scare me?

Black Hole: I think it's just my job.

Olivia: How do you feel about that?

Black Hole: Not so great. I feel a little cold. And I guess I feel a little lonely.

Olivia: So, if you are lonely, why do you do what you do? It doesn't sound like you enjoy it.

Black Hole: No, not really. Honestly, I've never thought about it. It's just who I am.

Olivia: Where do you live?

Black Hole: I live in your backyard right now but that can change. I'm beside you now.

Olivia: Okay. Can you move where you live to near my back fence so I don't run into you unexpectedly?

Black Hole: I guess I can do that.

Olivia: So why are you here? Are you trying to teach me something?

Black Hole: I'm trying to teach you that there are scary things in the world and that you must be careful.

Olivia: I know there are scary things in the world. I don't think I need you for that.

(The Black Hole shrugs and they sit in silence.)

Olivia: So how long have you been here?

Black Hole: I opened up when you got the news about your sister. You were pretty out of it then.

(Olivia notices she is getting upset and feels like ending the discussion.)

Olivia: Okay, thanks for talking. I feel like I want to take a break now.

Note that just as Olivia did, you have full control of the experience and can control the length, pace, and depth of the conversation.

Practice #3:
Ask, "What Can I Learn?"

The more you interact with your image, the more it might come to life. Your image may talk to you and offer new ideas or thoughts. Sometimes the image will answer verbally. Other times the image will reveal a message to you visually.

As it does so, I want you to stay open to the possibility of learning from your image.

Your image may offer you a direct message or it may try to communicate through emotions, colors, sound, or surrounding images. For example, your image may become sad, or you will notice that the image is in a different environment. Remember to have patience, as it may take time to understand what the image is trying to communicate. If you get confused, don your Curiosity Cap; a playful approach will make this experience more fun.

During your next conversation with your image, center yourself and repeat the breathing exercise. When you are ready, ask your image the following:

- Is there something you have been trying to tell me?
- What are you trying to teach me?
- Is there something you want to show me?

Take notes in your journal. Reflect on what you hear, see, feel, and what is happening with the image. Note details like colors, settings, sounds, and anything else that seems significant.

Olivia's Interview with Her Image (Dialogue #2)

About a week later Olivia decided to connect with her image again and go a little deeper. She imagined the two of them sitting at a park together:

Olivia: Hello again. Thanks for coming.

Black Hole: Yeah, no problem.

Olivia: You don't seem as scary today.

Black Hole: Huh.

Olivia: So, I guess I just don't understand why you're here. Are you trying to teach me something?

Black Hole: I'm here to teach you about the power of your fear. You are so scared of me. But you don't even know if I'm real.

Olivia: You feel real and look real. So, what is it that you want to show me about fear?

Black Hole: That it can take you down, control you, make you stop living. I think you may have stopped living a little bit, after your sister died.

Olivia: Hmmm, I guess in some ways I did. I stopped going out. I stopped accepting invitations to coffee or the movies. I just felt like a raw nerve. Like I would be hurt if I stepped outside.

Black Hole: What if that's not true?

Olivia: It might not be true. But hey, the way you look is scaring me. Would you mind closing up the hole and showing me some stable ground? I think that will help me feel like it's safe to go outside again, and that I won't get swallowed up.

The Black Hole was quiet for three minutes before it spoke again.

Black Hole: I can do that. I can make the ground stable.

Olivia watched as the Black Hole slowly closed and in its place was flat earth.

Olivia: Thank you. Thank you for coming to me, for showing me what I was afraid of.

* * *

Olivia was quite surprised that the image was helpful, and that it had a positive message for her. It took her months to start accepting invitations to go out, but the first time she did, she imagined the stable ground she saw when interacting with her image. Seeing the flat ground made her feel more secure to take that step.

Note that it may take several sessions to get to the place where your image is cooperative or helpful. Be patient with your process.

After-the-Practices Check-In

Just as you did before you tried the practices, it's time to look once again at the following questions.

1.   Is the image a positive force in my life?

_____

_____

_____

_____

2.   Is the image a neutral force in my life?

_____

_____

_____

_____

3.   Is the image a warning sign in my life?

_____

_____

_____

_____

As you answer the check-in questions, remember that your only goal is to become aware of your feelings. It can take time and patience for feelings to shift and for integration to occur. Allow yourself to be wherever you are without judgment.

Okay, let's take a moment to review your answers.

If you answered YES to "Is the image a positive force in my life?"

Allow yourself to drink in the good feelings. Ask yourself, *In what ways is that positivity showing up in my life? What kind of positive impact is it having on my life? How might it continue to be a growing force of positivity in my life?*

If you answered YES to "Is the image a neutral force in my life?"

Grab your journal and answer the following questions. How does neutral feel inside your body? Do you feel safe? Does it feel calming? Did the image have anything to say to you, or was it quiet? Write about your experience of the image being neutral.

If you answered YES to the question, "Is the image a warning sign in my life?"

No reason for concern. Warning signs can often be gentle nudges. The gentle nudge may suggest that you need more self-care, a trusted friend or therapist to lean on, or a little time away from processing your pain. Take some time to write in your journal. Ask yourself, *What kind of warning sign is this? Is it serious? Do I need to reach out for support right now?*

The integration process takes time. Feel free to repeat the practices as often as feels good or to modify them so they feel more natural to you.

Questions That May Arise

After doing this work for many years, I've noticed that people run into some similar sticking points when working on the Integrate It step. The following frequently asked questions can help you move gently through these sticking points and better understand the intuitive and internal process of grief integration.

Q: How do I know it's working, that integration is happening?

A: You will know that integration is happening because you will feel engaged, and your curiosity will be aroused. You may experience excitement, relief, or even discomfort. Yet, overall, you will know the process is working because, in some way, it feels helpful to you. Be patient and give it time. Pay attention to see if the process offers you any insight, if your awareness is growing, or if you feel a sense of movement. When looking back, most people who have engaged in this practice feel a sense of being more at ease with their loss.

Q: What if I don't feel the integration happening?

A: As you do this work, it's normal to wonder what may be happening under the surface. It's not always easy to track healing. Stay with it and give it some time. Try not to pressure yourself. Notice what feelings or thoughts are coming up. Also, observe how you generally feel in your life.

Q: What if I feel the image as a warning sign, and it scares me?

A: Remember that you are in control, and there is no rush. Trust your gut. You can always slow down or stop and take time for some needed self-care. Return to the work when you feel less triggered. If you want to continue, return to the "Make-it Real" physical practice. Draw your image or mold it using modeling clay. Turning your image into something physical helps to get the image out of your head. Sometimes continuing the process slowly and leaning into it, you may find that the fear is not real. For example, it might feel like a scary presence under the bed, but when you look, you find nothing there. Also, sometimes a scary image shows up to get your attention. If you are able and curious, try comforting the frightening image and see what happens. You may be surprised.

Q: What can I do if I need more self-care?

A: While doing this integration work, you may feel more tired than usual or even experience a sense of exhaustion on a more significant level. If you notice this, pay attention to what you see and hear. Listen to your own needs. Rest, curl up with a funny movie or a good book, make a cup of hot tea—anything that provides you with a sense of healing and comfort.

Q: What if I struggle with spending time or just "being with" my image?

A: Resistance to spending time with your image is normal. Again, pay attention to anything that's coming up for you without judgment. Are you feeling scared, repulsed, unsure, or confused? It's perfectly okay to acknowledge your struggle and see what happens next. Walk away for the day or a few days and try again when ready. Remember, this can be a playful act. If you had an imaginary friend as a child, try to recall what that was like.

Q: What if I struggle with meditation?

A: This struggle is common, so I encourage you to stay with it even if it is tough at first. There are many sources you can access to learn to meditate. You do not need to enter a deep meditative state. Just being conscious of your breath, your body, and the way you feel is enough.

Q: If I have turned my image into a physical form, how long should I keep it around?

A: This is up to you. Keep it around for however long it feels helpful. Some people create their image out of clay and keep it by their bedside permanently. Others draw it and then throw the drawing away. It's like any other relationship. Some stick around for a long time, while others come and go.

Q: What if I am still too sad or distressed?

A: You may need more time. Be with those feelings. Continue to use the imaginal technique to sit patiently with or dialogue with your grief. Be patient with yourself; if you are stuck reach out to a trusted friend or Grief Hack Buddy. If distress continues or gets worse immediately seek help from a mental health professional. If you start feeling hopeless, this is a signal to get help.

Q: What if I am encountering feelings of failure?

A: We all fail; it's part of the human condition. Failing is how we learn and how we learn resilience. There is no shame in failure. Feel your feelings and journal about them. Can you remember a time when you failed, faced your fears, and bounced back?

Q: What if the integration process feels messy or uncomfortable?

A: Then you're doing it right! There is no one clear path when doing this work. Messy is often the name of the game. Feeling a sense of discomfort can mean that something is happening internally. It may be hard to pinpoint, and you may feel impatient about wanting to feel better faster. Talk to yourself with kindness, encouraging yourself to engage with as much patience as possible. If you get confused, return to working with your intuition as your guide.

George and The Fire-Breathing Dragon

After sitting side by side with Red the dragon for a week, noticing the times that he felt anxious or uncomfortable, George reported that he felt ready for the step of integration.

First, he answered the check-in questions. He realized that, at times, he felt Red was a "not-so-great force in life." Sometimes Red felt like a warning sign, but mostly George just felt a sense of nervousness or fear when he thought about the dragon. Though he didn't always want to, he continued to sit with the image, and soon, he noticed a shift. Though the progress was sometimes very slight, he realized that he was becoming less afraid with each encounter. George also noticed that he was experiencing less fear and anxiousness and even felt neutral about Red at times.

After three weeks, he felt the urge to speak to Red in one of his "be with it" sessions.

He asked Red, "What is it that you want?"

To his surprise, Red stated, "Well, I like that you have been spending time with me. I think this is what I wanted."

George let out a laugh when he heard this. He then asked, "So, just spend time with you? Do I keep coming back?"

Red nodded and asked if George would mind being a regular visitor in Red's life. George nodded, agreeing to do so, and decided he would be happy to be a regular visitor.

The visit ended with Red extending his tail for George to touch.

* * *

I asked George how he felt when this happened. George told me he had an unexpected reaction: "I felt like I was not alone. I felt relieved and moved."

After this experience, George did the check-in questions and noticed that he was moving toward neutral feelings, and at times he found they were even a little positive.

He continued to visit Red. Soon their conversations took on a lighter tone. Sometimes George would even share his problems with Red. A few months later, after a tough day at work, George reported that as he walked to his car, he thought about calling a friend but decided to connect with Red first to see if he might help calm him down. George sat in his car and spoke with Red for about ten minutes. He found it did calm him down. When he called his friend, he noted how interesting it was that his first impulse when he struggled was to talk to Red.

Sarah and The Muddy Slime

Sarah started our session by saying, "Okay, I'm ready to talk to it." I told her it was courageous of her to allow herself to be in the presence of the slime ball.

Sarah took the slime from its package and put it on a paper plate she had brought from home. We looked at it together. She grounded herself, took several deep breaths, and began speaking to it. I asked her to write down the replies. This is the conversation she reported:

Sarah: Okay, why are you here?

Slime: Well, I guess I go wherever you go, really.

Sarah: Why?

Slime: I'm not sure; it just happens.

Sarah: Do you have anything to say to me?

Slime: Well, I'm glad you let me out because I don't really like it in the box.

Sarah: I think I felt safe to let you out because you were just a little bit of slime, but in my imagination, sometimes you can get as big as a house, and that scares me.

Slime: But you have the power to shrink me whenever you want.

Sarah: What do you mean?

Slime: Yeah, you can just use your Magic Wand, and then I shrink down to what is on that plate.

Sarah: Oh, I didn't know I could do that.

* * *

Sarah left that session feeling a great sense of relief.

For the next few weeks, she did some imaginative work with the box of slime. When the slime felt a little out of control, Sarah asked her father to sit with her and tap his finger on the box to calm it down. She watched how her father tapped on the box, and the next time it happened, she tapped on the box to calm it down.

She also continued to look at the play slime and reminded herself that she could always shrink the slime down to that smaller size.

Sarah thought about it momentarily, but the distrust and unease remained significant. She felt that she wasn't ready to let the slime out. And she was still nervous about him rocking the box.

I asked her if there was someone, dead or alive, that could help her.

"My dad, maybe."

"What do you think your dad can do?" I asked.

"I think if the slime starts rocking the box, he can grow tall and tap on the box until it calms down."

Sarah tried that technique, while imagining her father and asking him to tap on the box. She said it quieted down right away.

Sarah kept her father close in her imagination for a few weeks to help with the slime in a box. Then she realized she no longer needed her father's help. She could calm it down. She asked herself the check-in questions and found that, at this point, she was starting to feel that the slime was neutral, with only hints of fear here and there.

Then one day, she said she had a dream that the slime wanted out of its box, but in just little bits.

I asked her if she thought she could transform the slime when she let it out in little bits. She wondered what that might look like.

"What if you gave it a new texture or color?" I asked.

Thoughtfully she said, "I think I might be able to make it pink. But I am so unprepared to let it out, even in little bits."

For the next few weeks, Sarah imagined that she could change the color of the slime from a yucky greenish-brown to a soft pink. Once she had done that, she imagined that she could change the texture and decided it would move from that thick-sticky substance to a cloud-like texture.

Once the stuff in the box was pink and cloud-like, she didn't mind at all letting it out of the box, bit by bit.

Soon she looked forward to the moments when she could transform the slime into pink clouds. She loved watching the clouds float up into the sky and drift away. Sarah did this practice until she felt every bit of the slime was gone. She reported that, at times, she thought it would never go away completely.

One day as she walked to the park, she thought about how the slime had transformed.

She sat on the grass and watched the clouds, feeling a sense of peace she hadn't felt in years.

Jan and The Puzzle Pieces

Jan and I worked with her puzzle pieces for the next few months. She used her Curiosity Cap to continue to interview them, and then she used the Flowing Pen to write down what she'd learned. When she did the check-in questions, she noticed that she felt a sense of heaviness or deep sadness. She was sometimes scared that the heavy sadness might pull her into a depression. She noted that it was not positive or neutral and not really a warning sign but more like "a heavy weight attached to my body that might bring me down."

Late one night as Jan was getting ready for bed, she looked at the puzzle pieces glued to the plate by her bedside. As she climbed into bed, she said that she experienced a vivid moment of imagination, almost like a daydream, and allowed the scenario to play out. Here's what she reported:

"We were sitting in the back room of the restaurant laughing and hanging out like we used to. Then suddenly, I was alone with the glued-together puzzle pieces. There was one big puzzle piece, the corner piece, and it did the most talking. It was a sincere puzzle piece. I told the puzzle piece that I felt stupid for not being able to move on and that I often felt like crying.

"The big puzzle piece told me that I should cry and journal, that it was okay to cry because it knew how much I missed my restaurant family.

"Next, a smaller middle piece, colored red, spoke up. 'This is kind of like your childhood,' it said. I asked it what that meant.

"Then I suddenly felt like my journaling sessions brought up memories from my childhood. It was almost like I was watching a different daydream, sort of like a home movie. I was around nine, trying to do my math homework, knowing I was struggling and could not do it myself. I went around to each of my family members, asking for help. They either laughed at me or yelled at me to go away.

"Then I was back in the room with the red puzzle piece, and it spoke again, 'Stuff like that would happen to you all the time. When you needed an outfit for a dance recital, when you needed someone to come to the parent-teacher conference, when your sister forgot about your birthday, when your mom forgot to pick you up from camp.'

"I felt sick to my stomach. The red puzzle piece was correct. I suddenly remembered many times when I was a kid when I looked to my parents or sister for help, and they didn't show up. After this pattern repeated itself enough times, I concluded that no one was trustworthy—and that I could only depend on myself. Then I felt I sort of woke up, shaking myself out of the daydream.

"The next day I journaled about a moment at the restaurant when we were heavily overbooked, and I felt panicked and overwhelmed. Instead of sucking up my feelings and trying to do it all myself, I asked for help, and miraculously, everyone pitched in happily. I watched in amazement as each team member took over one of my problematic tasks or solved a problem. It was the first moment since childhood when I felt I could trust others.

"The memory made me want to reach out and connect with my former coworkers—and I wondered why I hadn't reached out before. I realized I was embarrassed to call because I had promised I would get a new job and try to hire them back so we could all be together again. But I had done the opposite: I found a new job and didn't contact them at all. I avoided calling them because it meant that our time together as a group was over—and I would have to move on. I was avoiding them because I didn't want to feel that loss."

Jan allowed herself to feel the loss in little bits. She hated crying but would allow herself a few tears here and there. She was surprised at how much relief she felt by acknowledging and feeling the pain.

"Then one day, I looked at my phone at an old text message and realized I wanted to reach out to an old friend from the restaurant. I started with just one text; she texted right back, saying she was missing me." After that, slowly, one by one, Jan began reaching out to the members of her restaurant family. She was initially nervous because she thought they might be upset with her for not contacting them earlier. But they were all happy to hear her voice.

A few of them went out for drinks, and Jan found she was deeply moved by seeing them again. She complained that her new coworkers kept her at a distance, and she felt lonely at work. Then a meaningful conversation happened.

One of her former coworkers, Marcel, told her that for the first three years at the restaurant, most of the employees felt that she was standoffish and hard to get to know. He said they often asked her to go out for lunch or drinks, and she would always decline. They considered her a loner. Then around the fourth year, she began to soften, letting them in little by little.

Marcel looked her in the eyes and asked, "Do you think you might be pushing them away too?"

Jan drove home, buzzing with this new realization. It wasn't them; it was her. The next day she asked one of the coworkers at her new job if they would like to go to lunch. The co-worker expressed surprise, saying Jan usually had to work through lunch. Jan said she was going to try to shift away from that practice. The two went to lunch, and a few other coworkers joined them. Jan felt awkward initially, but by the end of the lunch, she felt herself relaxing and even laughing at some situations they'd all encountered at work.

That night she had a dream where new puzzle pieces seemed to fly toward each other, making an entirely new puzzle picture.

* * *

Take a moment to pat yourself on the back for moving through the Integrate It step. Chances are you have felt anxious or had upsetting thoughts during this process. But with patience and perseverance, you have opened your arms to the complex and often avoidable emotions of loss and grief.

You have embraced your lost loved ones in the present by weaving them into life and celebrating their memories. You have embarked on a method to accept losses and use them to move forward. You have likely wanted to turn back at times, and here you are.

Takeaways from Chapter Three

- Integrating It means interacting with our grief until it's just another part of ourselves.
- This process can be both challenging and rewarding.
- Working on the Integrate It step can help you to feel less fearful, sad, or anxious. You may experience increased awareness, a sense of emotional strength, release, relief, or healing.
- The Integrate It process is often intuitive and requires checking in with your gut feelings.
- The three Integrate It practices are:

  - Invite Your Image to Interact With You
  - Interview Your Image
  - Learn from Your Image

- We can keep lost loved ones alive in our lives by sharing memories with others who loved them.
- You will know you've integrated your loss when your image has become part of yourself, and you no longer feel scared to interact.
- Use the following three check-in questions before and after the practices to help track how your feelings may change toward your image.

Check-In Questions

- Is the image a positive force in my life?
- Is the image a neutral force in my life?
- Is the image a warning sign in my life?

Chapter Four:
Harness It

See It → I am aware of my grief.

Embrace It → Instead of running, I lean into my grief.

Integrate It → I interact with my grief until it's just another part of myself.

Harness It → My grief is now fueling my growth.

In the previous step, Integrate It, we took time to interact with our Grief-Imagic images until we felt they were just another part of our lives. Hopefully, you have moved from where the pain may have felt throbbing and active, to where it feels softer and more manageable. It's still there, but it doesn't hold the same power over you that it might once have had. It might even feel neutral, or better yet, it might be calling to you because it has some meaningful information to share.

Let's take a moment to review what has happened on your Grief-Imagic journey so far.

You have already come face to face with your grief. You have been willing to embrace it. I'm guessing this process has helped you understand your strength and resilience. While being with your grief, your fear has most likely diminished. Instead of running from it, you have befriended it and made it part of your life by integrating your loss into your life.

Our last step is the harnessing of the loss. During this step, I ask you to look at your life experiences and use them to enrich your life and perhaps the lives of others. You may not have considered yourself to be someone who might influence or inspire others. Now, you can put what you have learned into helpful service. You can do this in a personal, intimate way, meaning it's something just for you. Or you can bring what you've learned to another person, group, or to members of your community. Your words and actions can influence others in ways that may surprise and delight you.

I'm asking you to go inside and see yourself in this new light. Imagine that your small actions create ripples that impact the world. You may already be doing this in your world, possibly without intending to do so. During the Harness It step, we'll be exploring several ways that you can transform pain into positive energy.

There are many ways to use this transforming energy, from writing in a journal to changing personal habits, to getting healthier, to creating tangible items like art, or even starting a movement or a group.

Reasons We Harness It

- To use our grief experiences as fuel in our lives to do or create
- To give back to the community
- To better understand our growth process
- To better understand the profound strengths we may have just discovered
- To unearth and appreciate parts of ourselves that are ready to be expressed
- To share what we have learned and inspire others
- To expand our knowledge, hearts, and abilities to enrich our world

In my work, I've seen how people have interpreted this step in its many forms.

Nikki realized she wanted a deeper understanding of death after losing her mother. She began a spiritual journey and ended up becoming a Buddhist practitioner. Mara lived through losing her son to a rare form of cancer; she ended up starting an online support forum for parents of children with cancer. Rick, who got back on his feet after being homeless for six months, now volunteers at a homeless shelter. After going through a traumatic car accident, Ivan decided to quit his job as an accountant and pursue his lifelong dream of being a musician. Dana found meditation. Arlene found gardening. Sam became a wilderness guide for the forestry service.

What's Going on in Our Brains During the Harness It Stage

Let's return to the work of Mary Francis O'Connor. In her book, *The Grieving Brain: The Surprising Science on How We Learn from Love and Loss,* she discusses what happens in your brain when you lose someone you love. Your brain was mapped out in a certain way. When your loved one was alive and you searched for them, you were able to find them. You would call and they would pick up. But when the loved one passes, your brain can no longer find the person, and consequently, for a period your brain may get stuck on "find." Your brain is thinking, *I must find that person.* But then, you pick up the phone to call but there's no one to call. When we don't find our loved one, we can experience feelings of pain, confusion, and overwhelm.

When you're in the Harness It stage, your brain may become engaged with something new (like a project or artistic endeavor). Therefore, in this stage there are many opportunities to rewire our brains. You will spend less time trying to find the old relationship and more time searching for understanding or meaning. You may also spend time in the act of creating something new, which will come with a new, profound sense of gratitude. In the Harness It stage we open ourselves up to exploration, creativity, and sharing information. In this stage the brain is rewiring itself, and therefore creating a new, unique map. Also, your ability to do this is a result of all the previous work you have done. You now have emotional space available to start looking at life anew.

A bit about my story: As mentioned earlier, I lost both parents before the age of eight. Though it took many years, I embarked on a spiritual and creative journey when I reached the Harness It stage. I took classes, engaged in art workshops, studied dream and active imagination and interpretation, and explored spiritual practices. Yet I always felt this calling to share the parts of writing my story that could help people. I decided to write it down for others. As I began to write, I discovered how vital writing felt for me. I realized I wanted to get it down for myself. I understood that my life could have taken a different turn. I might have shut down emotionally and never fully experienced that part of my personality. My profound losses at such an early age hindered my emotional growth and expression. They may have stopped me from growing. But somehow, I was able to move through my grief and find another side. I wanted to share that experience, and it eventually became *Six Healing Questions: A Gentle Path to Facing Childhood Loss of a Parent*. Writing the book was powerful and freeing. Putting it out into the world taught me endless lessons about the power of harnessing my experiences. No matter how you choose to Harness It, I'm hoping you will walk with open eyes, embrace patience, and be ready to unearth new and powerful discoveries about yourself.

Going Forward with Your Grief-Imagic Image

As we move into the Harness It step, your image gets to play a new role. No longer haunting or troublemaking, your image can now be an ongoing source of comfort, insight, and inspiration. Remember that this is a result of following the steps and engaging in the practices in the previous chapters. You have done a lot of hard work. In the practices below, you'll be working with your image to help you understand better how you are growing from this challenging process. Your image may help you see new possibilities for your life, ways to turn your grief into something creative, productive, and resourceful.

An example is Eva. She lost her husband and her beloved home of twenty-five years, all in six months. Her image was a massive crater-like hole that she had fallen into. The crater kept her alone and cut off from the world for several years. By working through the steps, the dark crater transformed into a cozy cave to heal and hibernate. When she was ready for the Harness It stage, Eva would sit in the cozy cave for ideas. During one of her times in the cave, she came up with the idea of bringing meals to seniors living on their own who needed company. Eva felt that she, more than anyone, understood loneliness. In this way she turned this idea into reality. She harnessed her pain and transformed it into a new life path—a path that turned out to be one of the most rewarding chapters of her life.

You may find yourself turning your grief into:

- Art (writing, sculpture, collage, garden)
- Cooking
- A purpose
- Work
- Doing research
- Planning a trip
- Creating a foundation
- Finding what is funny about the situation
- Dance / movement
- Rock collecting (or any collecting)
- Pottery

Did You Know?

Did you know that creating art can help you view your world in new ways, release emotions, and enhance your brain? Susan Magsamen and Ivy Ross, researchers and authors of *Your Brain on Art: How the Arts Transforms Us,* show that creating art—such as crafting, drawing, painting, and writing—improves your cognitive abilities. It's not about being artistically talented or crafting with a specific result in mind. It's about "the doing," the practice of being artistic at any level. Studies also show that these artistic pursuits are strengthening connections in our brains and helping to create new neural pathways.

Your Image May Change Form or Turn into a New Image

Images may come and go. Some may stay with you as trusted friends. Others may disappear when no longer needed or morph into a new image as your relationship with your loss changes. Nothing to be concerned about, just good to notice. Put on your Curiosity Cap and observe.

Jose's original image was a shark-dragon creature. As he continued to work with it in the Harness It stage, he discovered that it had turned into a playful octopus that could change colors. He said that the shift happened one day when he set up a time to talk. In his mind, he met the shark/dragon at the shore, where it then it jumped in, and Jose followed him in the water. When Jose opened his eyes underwater, he saw the creature morph into the playful octopus. He noted that he experienced relief while watching the transformation. He found the octopus a lot less threatening and enjoyed spending time with it underwater.

If your image changes, pick up the Flowing Pen and write about it in your journal. How has it changed? What does this mean to you?

Practice #1:
Going to the Movies with Your Image

By the time you reached the Integrate It stage, your image had transformed into something less threatening and became just another aspect of your life. As we talked about in chapter three, your image may express that it has lessons teach you. In fact, your image might become an ongoing source of new thoughts and ideas. So, what if you took it to the movies?

Imagine sitting in a comfortable movie theater, eating popcorn next to your image. Bring any questions you have to the forefront of your mind. Ask your image a question. Any question. For example, you could ask, "What else do you think I have to learn from this situation?" Or, "Is there anything else you want to share with me?" Or, "How do you see me moving forward now?"

Your image may answer you verbally, or it may answer you visually. If it provides visual images, all you do is watch the movie.

Take a moment to notice what you see, what you hear, or what may be unfolding before you.

During this practice, it's essential to be open and to have patience. Understanding what your image is trying to tell you may take time.

Write down your observations in your journal with the Flowing Pen. Feel free to repeat this with your image as many times as you would like.

After you've asked all your questions and the movie has finished take some time to reflect. What was the most powerful thought, idea, or message you received?

_____

_____

_____

_____

_____

_____

_____

Grief Hack

Practice #2:
What You Might Say to a Friend

In this Harness It practice, you will learn to talk to yourself as you might speak to a beloved friend. The reason to do this practice is to give yourself a different perspective; we are often harder on ourselves than on the people we love. This practice can help quiet your inner critic and cultivate an attitude of self-kindness.

Imagine that a good friend has come to talk to you about an upsetting loss—similar to yours—that happened a few years back. You offer them a seat and a cup of coffee or tea. They're curious to know your thoughts and observations on how they've been transformed through grief. You listen and offer feedback about how this loss has changed them and impacted their life.

What would you say? How might you see your friend as a changed person—possibly stronger, smarter, braver, or more empathetic? Take a moment to express what you might say and how you might comfort this friend.

Now answer the following questions:

- How did you feel about your friend as you wrote this?
- Did you gain any insight about perspectives on the loss?
- Do you think your friend would have felt better after hearing what you had to say?

_____

_____

_____

_____

_____

_____

Practice #3:
See It as a Spiky Precious Gem

Think back on a memory that feels hurtful or prickly related to a loss. Allow that moment to play out in your mind. While you may have colored this moment as a dark or upsetting experience, what if you decided, just for a bit, to think of this moment as a precious gem with spiky edges, like a diamond or a geode.

The memory has "spiky edges" because it still may hurt to look at it. But know that there is something precious inside this memory, something that may be able to provide you fuel for your life.

Ask yourself:

- How is this memory a gift?
- Is there anything good that can come out of this memory?
- Did this moment provide me with any insight, courage, or understanding?

_____

_____

_____

_____

_____

_____

_____

_____

_____

_____

Make Some Creative Mistakes

Is there anything creative you have always wanted to try but have not yet tried? Remember: you don't need to have the skills right not—it's not about the product but your experience.

Some ideas to consider include painting, dancing, scrapbooking, mosaic making, cooking, candle making, watercolor, fencing, karate, tai chi, gardening, making videos, knitting, playing an instrument, sculpting, working out, dancing, graphic design, collecting, traveling, or writing.

The Harness It stage is a great time to try!

Other Ways to Harness It

Besides being creative or doing any of the activities we just considered, review a few other ways to practice the Harness It phase. Remember that you should only do something once you feel ready. It shouldn't feel like pressure, but more like an extension of your growing spirit.

- Find your community—join an organization related to your loss/grief
- Volunteer for an organization related to your loss/grief
- Start an "in the name of" or "in memory of" campaign—it could be a hiking group, a letter-writing group, a lobbying group, or a charity organization
- Talk to kids/universities about how your experience has transformed you
- Plant a garden or create an altar
- Find a spot in nature to travel to (maybe someplace that holds meaning or inspires you)
- Start your own organization

- Write a tribute letter and consider submitting it for publication in a relevant magazine or website
- Write your memoir or a short story about your experience
- Start a dream journal
- Donate to a cause
- Contribute to the cause of legal justice by writing to a congressperson or working to change a law
- Embrace a social justice issue
- Find a spiritual home or practice

Questions That May Arise

Q: Is my image the wisest part of myself trying to communicate with me?

A: It's possible (and maybe even probable) that your image is the wisest part of you trying to communicate with you. The way that I look at it is, either way, the process works. If it's not the wisest part of you, the process and your image can still offer you incredible insight, awareness opportunities. and growth.

Q: What if I don't feel like harnessing my grief?

A: Experiencing any level of personal growth may be enough for you. Or you may discover a way to harness it later in your grief journey. Being aware and opening yourself to the possibility creates space. You may surprise yourself. Check in with your image from time to time to see if there is any wise direction coming your way.

Q: What if I still feel my image as threatening or saddening?

A: Each person's process is different. Depending on the loss and how it impacted your life, it may take longer for it to not seem negative to you. Feel good about your insight and creativity to date. There is no exact schedule. You are unique, and whatever is happening is best for you. Another option is to go back and repeat the work suggested in the earlier chapters.

Q: What if I feel like I want to move forward but don't get a clear message from my image?

A: Give yourself time. Breathe. Relax. It will come to you when you're ready. Keep your Curiosity Cap handy and put it on from time to time.

George and the Fire-Breathing Dragon

After realizing that he could visit and even speak to Red for a sense of comfort, George found himself in regular contact, seeing Red about two or three times a week.

One day at work, George was cleaning out his desk and found a postcard that he and his cousin Dale had bought during a road trip to the Grand Canyon. Out of nowhere, George felt hit in the gut, like he wanted to cry. He decided to go to his car and try the "going to the movies" practice to speak with Red.

George imagined sitting in a comfortable movie theater, eating popcorn next to Red. George expressed to Red that he was frustrated because he was still grieving the loss of his cousin, and he had hoped he'd be over it by now. George asked Red, "Why do I feel so much pain today?" and, "What else do you think I have to learn from this situation?"

He reported the conversation went like this.

George: This is ridiculous. Dale died over two years ago, and I find a postcard, and suddenly I can't function.

Red: You will always miss Dale. You may get triggered like this from time to time because one never really gets over a loss—it's more like you learn to live side by side with it.

George: Finding that postcard just reminded me that I am living my life without my best friend. I feel alone.

Red: It's good to notice that.

George: Yeah, okay, I notice it. So now what?

Red: It seems like you're really missing some companionship.

George: It's that, and it's the adventure. Dale and I used to take these long, crazy road trips. But lately, I haven't gone anywhere. I just don't feel like I have the energy.

Red: What if you took a road trip in honor of your experiences with Dale? What if you visited a few of his favorite spots?

George thought for a while after this conversation. A week later, he decided to drive up to Big Sur, one of their favorite destinations. While driving, he remembered how he and Dale would sit side by side and joke, listen to music, and watch the scenery roll by. George ached with loneliness. He thought about the spiky gem questions:

How are my memories a gift? Is there anything good that can come out of those memories?

What came to George as he drove was that his time with Dale was like a mirror that revealed the best parts of himself. He realized what a gift Dale had given him: to be an explorer in the world, driving to wacky places and starting conversations with strangers.

When George got home from the trip, he called as many family members as possible and told them he'd be organizing an annual family reunion that would include a road trip to a new destination each year. About four months later, George and three of his cousins took a road trip to a mountain town in Colorado that George had always wanted to see. George had a fantastic time and began to feel that a bit of Dale was within him, inspiring him and pushing him to be an explorer of the Earth once again.

Now, the four cousins gather each year on Dale's birthday and throw a pin on a map. Wherever the pin lands, that's their destination. George commented that though the ache for his best friend never went away, Dale's spirit feels as strong as ever inside him when he's on the road.

Sarah and The Muddy Slime

When Sarah was ready to let the slime out of the box, she did so in little bits. She practiced imagining the greasy mud-colored slime turning into the texture of a light cloud, then turning a lovely color of pink, almost sunset colored.

I asked her how she might incorporate the light pink cloud material into her life in a way that felt positive. At first, she could think of nothing, then she said, "If I put the pink clouds in the sky, that feels good."

She was quiet momentarily, then added, "Maybe I could see the light pink clouds as my mom and dad looking down on me and smiling?"

Upon seeing that image in her mind's eye, Sarah suddenly felt her body relax in a way she said she hadn't experienced in years. She also began to cry. Usually, Sarah would stop herself from crying but this time she let the tears flow. She understood that she was crying because when she imagined the pink cloud, she felt the kind of warmth that felt like getting a hug from her mother. She realized she'd been aching for that feeling.

For the next few weeks, Sarah worked on allowing the brown slime out in little bits and then enjoyed watching it transform into light, fluffy pink cloud hugs. A few weeks later, Sarah realized there was no more slime left in the box. She was a bit shocked. There had been a time when she thought she would never see the end of the slime.

A few weeks later, she confessed that when she missed her mom and wanted to feel calm, she beat herself up internally for "being so weak."

To combat this thought, Sarah imagined that her good friend Ellen had come to talk to Sarah about the loss of her parents. Sarah imagined how she would treat Ellen kindly, offering her tea and a warm blanket.

Sarah imagined what she would say to Ellen, noting how easy it was to be warm, caring, accepting, and supportive when it came to her friend's feelings.

She told Ellen, "When you feel insecure, what if you looked up into the sky and talked to imaginary pink clouds?"

This suggestion sent a calm wave throughout her whole body. Sarah felt lighter, more at ease.

She later shared with me, "Honestly, the pink clouds are near me a lot, and well, they are comforting to me in a way I could never have dreamed."

Sarah thought that was the end of the journey with her slime. She loved finding pink clouds in the sky and would often sit underneath them, allowing a sense of closeness with her parents. She began to think about her mother, who had started a reading program at the school where she'd taught struggling kids at risk of being left behind.

Sarah decided to try the "going to the movies" practice. She sat beside the pink clouds and asked them,

What else do you think I have to learn from this situation? Is there anything else you want to share with me? How do you see me moving forward now?

Then she sat back and watched the movie screen come to life. It was a movie about a life experience Sarah had a few years earlier. She was visiting her mother at the school and helping with her students. Sarah noticed a profound, almost sacred sense of joy on her mother's face as she worked with the kids.

A couple of days later, Sarah found herself driving to the same school and just sitting outside. Then she found herself in conversation with the clouds once again. They urged her to go inside, as if asking her to continue the program her mother had created. Sarah listened to this quiet intuition, and for reasons she could not explain, she went inside the school, asked to speak to the principal, and asked if she could continue the struggling reader program in honor of her mother.

The principal was overcome with emotion. It turns out the school staff had been talking about her mother just that week, about how much they missed her, and about the three little girls at the school who desperately needed her help.

Sarah met with the girls the next day. Sitting at the desk, she felt her mother's spirit infuse her with boldness, ability, and purpose. Sarah worked with the girls all year long. She said the work, which grew into a volunteer program that included fourteen parents, was probably some of the most rewarding work she had ever done.

Now, when Sarah sees a pink cloud, she looks up and thanks her parents for giving her this opportunity to create something so unexpected and fulfilling.

Jan and The Puzzle Pieces

Jan reported feeling much relief just by acknowledging the emotions surrounding the loss of her restaurant family. She also felt quite a bit of sadness; by getting in touch with her former coworkers, she found out something that shocked her: they had all moved on! The dream of getting everyone back together would never come true.

Jan noted that she became depressed for a few days after accepting this. She didn't want to get up, go outside, or eat much. Then she remembered the question her former co-worker Marcel had asked her, and pondered: *Was she pushing away her new coworkers, like she did with her original coworkers? Did her new coworkers view her as a not-so-friendly loner?*

At first, Jan started to beat herself up for being closed off, repeating past mistakes, and pushing people away. Then she decided to use the practice, "What would I say to a friend?" Jan thought about it and realized that if a friend came to her and shared her struggle, she'd be compassionate and understanding. She would remind her friend that she'd grown up in a family that didn't foster trust and taught her to depend only on herself. Jan felt calmer, treating herself in this more loving manner. When she drove to work the following day, she realized she was just sad, and that was that. Sad, lonely for her old crew, and upset by the realization that that special time in her life was indeed over. She allowed herself to cry and told herself it was okay to feel her emotions.

At lunchtime that same day, Jan could feel something calling to her, nagging at her. She wondered if it was the puzzle pieces. She took some time at a small park near work to take her puzzle pieces to the movies.

As she sat in the movie theater with her puzzle pieces, she noticed that she felt a kind of nervous energy. She asked the puzzle pieces the question, *How do you see me moving forward now?*

Jan then let the movie play out. She saw herself on screen at a crossroads. If she went in one direction, she saw herself diving into a time of sadness and loneliness. But if she went in the other direction, she saw herself walking around a corner. Still feeling sad and a bit lonely, she saw herself on screen, turning the corner where she came face to face with the big puzzle piece. It held a sign that read, "Just be open to what may come."

At the end of the week, Carmen, the new coworker she was closest to at her HR job, said to her, "I won't bother asking you to lunch again, but let me know if you want me to bring something back."

A light bulb went off. Jan had been pushing people away. It had been unintentional, like muscle memory, almost. Jan told her coworker that she would love to go to lunch.

At lunch, Jan asked Carmen for insight. How was Jan seen by the rest of her co-workers? Carmen said that most people in the office felt like she was a little cold and standoffish. She shared with Jan that it seemed like every few weeks, she'd say something like, "I'm just doing my time at HR until I can get back to the restaurant business." Jan shared her insights with Carmen and asked if Carmen would keep joining her for lunch. Carmen happily agreed.

Later that night, when Jan was getting ready for bed, she felt another pull to listen to her puzzle pieces. She sat on her couch and returned to the movie theater with them.

As the movie played, she noticed the puzzle pieces were changing shape and color. She said they were all very talkative, almost all at once. I asked her what they said to her.

"Well, one said that it was okay to let go of my old restaurant family— that they would still be there for me, but it would look different than it did before."

Then the image of all her old coworkers at dinner popped on the screen. This image made Jan remember Marcel's idea that the restaurant family should all meet for a monthly dinner so they could keep in touch.

Then, another puzzle piece asked her to admit that she was good at her job in HR and that maybe, HR suited her better than restaurant management. But the problem was that, at times, she lacked empathy for others.

The puzzle piece told her she could move up in the company if she was brave enough to look at the empathy issue and allow herself to make new friends.

The last puzzle piece was the most interesting. It said that her loss, her sadness about losing that original family of restaurant coworkers, could be the missing ingredient. If she could remember how that felt and not push it away, she could more readily access empathy for others. Then she saw herself on the movie screen once again, only this time sitting with an employee at the HR office, expressing empathy and concern.

Jan was changed by this experience with her puzzle pieces. She began using her experience of losing her restaurant family in her new HR career as a tool to connect to grief that her new coworkers might be feeling for one reason or another. She realized that she did understand more about employee relationships, having a sense of a work family, tackling loss, and the importance of communication and nurturing relationships.

Takeaways from Chapter Four

- Harnessing It means looking at your experiences to see if you can use them to enrich your life and perhaps the lives of others.
- The reason we Harness It is so that we can unearth and appreciate parts of ourselves that are ready to be expressed, or to give back to our community.
- What you may discover about your Grief-Imagic image is that it's no longer haunting or troublemaking.
- Your image may now be an ongoing source of comfort, insight, and inspiration.
- Examples of ways you may Harness It: journal/write it down, find your tribe, create art, explore an aspect of your spirituality, or join a social justice movement or environmental campaign to make life better.

The three practices that can help you to Harness It:

- "Going to the movies" with Your Image. This helps you to answer the question, *Is there anything else I need to learn from the experience?*
- What You Might Say to a Friend. This helps you to see if you can gain any insight or perspectives on the loss.
- See it as Spiky Precious Gem. Ask, *How is this memory a gift?* This helps you to recognize ways the memory of this loss has made you stronger, more fulfilled, more empathetic, or more resilient.

Closing

Dear Reader,

It's time to say goodbye. I will miss you, my readers, who are my inspiration and my muse.

I want to take a moment to thank you for joining me on this creative, healing journey. Your willingness to explore your loss and try these practices shows that you are open to living your life to the fullest. You have practiced your observation skills about your feelings and your physical reactions to loss. You have engaged your imagination in new ways and come face to face with your grief. You've leaned into your grief and embraced it. You have taken steps to integrate your grief into your life. As you go forward and harness your grief, you have the joy of experiencing the transformation and beauty that grows from your work with the experience of loss.

Doing this work gives you an edge, or what I refer to in the title of this book, a grief hack. It's playful imaginative way to help you reduce your suffering and open to new horizons. By allowing this process to become part of your life, you are changed forever. Yes, loss may still be scary. Remember that it's healthy to acknowledge and allow your feelings. That's just part of being human. The difference is that once you are well versed in your Grief-Imagic tools, you're no longer at the mercy of fear and the pain of loss. When loss pops up (as we know it inevitably will), you now have tools. Most importantly, you will know how to walk yourself through the steps of See It, Embrace It, Integrate It, and Harness It. If you find yourself lost, overwhelmed, or stuck while using the Grief-Imagic process, you can call on your Magic Wand, Curiosity Cap, and Flowing Pen. You may find that the more you use your tools, the more you understand that yes, loss and grief change your life. You may have to live with loss, but you don't need to suffer forever because of the loss. You can become stronger, more resilient—even more joyful.

The wonderful knowledge you now possess is that:

- You know you will encounter grief and loss again in life—yet you also know there are gifts to be found in grief (what I like to call the "spiky gems").
- You know that you have solid, concrete tools to help you through the loss.

While I would never wish my own story of early loss on anyone, it has transformed my life in unexpected and astonishing ways. Now it's your turn to continue your creative and transformative journey.

The Uses of Sorrow

Someone I loved once gave me

a box full of darkness.

It took me years to understand

that this, too, was a gift.

−Mary Oliver, American poet

Acknowledgments

My older brothers who lovingly cared for me as a child.

Maure Quilter for her love, understanding, and mentoring.

Marni Freedman for so many things I could write a whole book about. Her professional help and guidance in writing about mental health has been invaluable as well as being my editor and coach.

Gina Simmons for writing my foreword.

Our amazing San Diego writing community for support.

Shout out to the International Memoir Writers Association.

About the Author
Madonna Treadway

Madonna was born in a rural area in North Dakota, the youngest of four children. Being the only girl with three older brothers and loving parents, she felt life was near perfect. However, by the age of eight, her young life would be turned upside down. At six, her mother died of breast cancer, and just one year later, her father took his life after struggling with the effects of a massive stroke. The family moved on the only way they knew how. They never looked back. They tucked away all their grief to find the strength to move on.

In her forties, Madonna was a successful corporate executive, yet she found herself struggling with intimate relationships and a sense of deep disconnection to her life. It was at this time that she began to explore what happened to her as a child. She looked at what had been tucked away so many years earlier to see the impact it had on her adult life.

Researching and writing about early loss led her to a path of understanding and connection to her rich inner life. She found new ways of connecting to her emotions, which allowed her to connect with others in new and profound ways. Soon, Madonna began to offer hope and community to others who had walked a similar path. She was able to see in them, what she had locked away for years—the potential for a full and vibrant life. Today, Madonna is a guide who has truly walked the unusual and difficult path of healing and transforming her grief and can offer unique insight for anyone on this journey seeking hope, growth, or healing.

For the last twenty-five years, Madonna (BS, MBA) has owned an ongoing speaking and consulting business with her husband, Bob. Her career includes teaching at the high school and university level and time spent as an executive who managed both clients and acquisitions and sales nationally before joining Bob in their current venture. She also continues to look for ways that her writing can support others who have experienced loss.

Madonna's award-winning book *Six Healing Questions* was published in 2019. She was a winner of the San Diego Memoir Writers Association's 2018 Memoir Showcase, which featured her story entitled "Secrets." She is a guest blogger for The Feisty Writer. Her work was featured in the 2019 anthology Shaking the Tree Volume Two: brazen. short. memoir. She has been featured on panels at the San Diego Writers Festival for several years.

Madonna is a member of the San Diego Memoir Writers Association and plays an active role in the writing community. What makes Madonna unique is her empathy for all those who suffer from loss. This along with her attitude about facing loss without fear and sharing ways to transform loss is an inspiring combination.

Her personal passions are human rights, animal well-being, literacy, and the arts. She is a world traveler, past marathon runner, and an avid wine enthusiast.

She lives in San Diego with her husband. Over the last few years, she experienced the loss of her two beloved animal companions, Abby and Auggie. Another fluffy companion will be joining their family soon.

To connect with Madonna, visit
MadonnaTreadway.com

Works Cited

Daniel, Terri. Grief and God: When Religion Does More Harm Than Healing. Alresford: John Hunt Publishing, 2019.

Johnson, Robert A. Inner Work: Using Dreams and Active Imagination for Personal Growth. San Francisco: Harper San Francisco, 1989.

Jung, C. G., and Aniela Jaffé. Memories, Dreams, Reflections. New York: Vintage Books/Random House, 1989.

Lewis, C. S., A Grief Observed. San Francisco: Harper Collins, 2001.

Liebenow, Mark. "Hiking in Yosemite as Grief Therapy." The Good Men Project, August 28, 2021. https://goodmenproject.com/featured-content/hiking-in-yosemite-as-grief-therapy-wcz/.

Magsamen, Susan and Ivy Ross. Your Brain on Art: How the Arts Transform Us. New York: Random House, 2023.

Marshall, Lisa. "Your Brain on Imagination: It's a Lot Like the Real Thing, Study Shows," CU Boulder Today, December 11, 2018, https://www.colorado.edu/today/node/31511.

O'Connor, Mary Francis. The Grieving Brain: The Surprising Science on How We Learn from Love and Loss. New York: Harper Collins, 2023.

Pennebaker, James. Opening Up by Writing it Down: How Expressive Writing Improves Health and Eases Emotional Pain. New York: The Guilford Press, 2016.

Reddan, Marianne Cumella, Tor Dessart Wager, and Daniela Schiller. "Attenuating Neural Threat Expression with Imagination." Neuron 100, 4 (November 2018): 994, https://doi.org/10.1016/j.neuron.2018.10.047.

Simmons Schneider, Gina. Frazzlebrain: Break Free from Anxiety, Anger, and Stress Using Advanced Discoveries in Neuropsychology. Las Vegas: Central Recovery Press, 2022.

Treadway, Madonna, Six Healing Questions: A Gentle Path to Facing Childhood Loss of a Parent. San Diego: MCM, 2019.

Thank You for Reading

If you enjoyed this book, please take a few moments to write a review on Amazon and GoodReads. Thank you!

You can also visit my website at MadonnaTreadway.com

Follow me on Facebook: Facebook.com/Madonna.Treadway

Follow me on Instagram: @madonnatreadway

Book Club Questions for
Grief Hack: A Creative Process for Transforming Loss

- What motivated your group to choose this book?
- How has *Grief Hack* changed your approach to loss and your ability to transform it into something healing and helpful?
- Were there any big surprises as you used the Grief-Imagic steps to transform your grief?
- Do you look at grief differently now? What's the biggest change?
- What does your Magic Wand look like? How about your Curiosity Cap?
- What did it feel like using your Flowing Pen?
- During the See It step, describe the first image that came to mind?
- As you worked through the four steps, did you identify losses you weren't aware you were holding on to?
- What lessons did you learn from one or more of your images?
- During the "make it real" practice, what object did you find as a physical representation of your grief? How did it feel to hold it in your hands?
- During the Harness It step, did you notice how your experience of transforming your loss enriched your life? Has it enriched the lives of your close family, friends, or greater community?

- Do you feel stronger and more resilient after reading the book and working through the four steps?
- Do you feel the practices in *Grief Hack* encourage self-compassion and self-care? Please say more about this if you feel it is true.

Printed in the USA
CPSIA information can be obtained
at www.ICGtesting.com
JSHW010844210324
59608JS00013B/61

9 781959 793014